SCOTLAND
Through the Ages

Written and photographed by
Michael Jenner

A MERMAID BOOK

by the same author
LONDON HERITAGE

MICHAEL JOSEPH LTD

Published by the Penguin Group
27 Wrights Lane, London W8 5TZ, England
Viking Penguin Inc., 40 West 23rd Street, New York, New York 10010, USA
Penguin Books Australia Ltd, Ringwood, Victoria, Australia
Penguin Books Canada Ltd, 2801 John Street, Markham, Ontario, Canada L3R 1B4
Penguin Books (NZ) Ltd, 182-190 Wairau Road, Auckland 10, New Zealand

Penguin Books Ltd, Registered Offices: Harmondsworth, Middlesex, England

First published in Great Britain May 1987
First published in Mermaid Books 1989
Text and illustrations copyright © Michael Jenner 1987
Maps by Boris Weltman

British Library Cataloguing in Publication Data

Jenner, Michael, *1946–*
    Scotland through the ages.
    1. Scotland—History
    I. Title
    941.1   DA760

ISBN 0 7181 2681 5

Printed in Spain by Graficromo

Loch Moidart

Contents

Acknowledgements

The research involved in the preparation of *Scotland Through the Ages* took me the length and breadth of the country and I was fortunate to enjoy the help and co-operation of a vast number of people. I would like to thank the National Trust for Scotland for the kind assistance I always received from many individuals at the properties of the Trust throughout the country. Valuable help was also given by the Nature Conservancy Council (especially on the Isle of Rhum), the Scottish Tourist Board, the Highlands and Islands Development Board, the Orkney Tourist Organisation, the Shetland Tourist Organisation, British Rail, the Burrell Collection, the Hunterian Museum, the Glasgow School of Art, Glasgow City Chambers, Huntly House Museum in Edinburgh, and the owners and custodians of Abbotsford, Blair, Drumlanrig, Dunrobin, Floors, Glamis, Kinloch Castle and Scone. Special mention should be made of the Ancient Monuments Division of the Scottish Development Department, whose painstaking care of Scotland's oldest sites and ruins was a constant source of pleasure. Finally, I should like to acknowledge the debt I owe to the many writers, some listed in the bibliography, whose works have inspired in me a deep affection for Scotland, the land and its people.

The photos on pages 62 and 63 are reproduced by permission of the Hunterian Museum of the University of Glasgow, and those on pages 243 and 244 by permission of the Burrell Collection, Glasgow Museums and Art Galleries.

To Diana, with love

Introduction

The harshness of much of Scotland's terrain makes a direct, personal appeal to the senses, unlike the softer, prettier contours to be encountered south of the border, which may be enjoyed with more detachment. Scotland's heroic past, rugged grandeur and idiosyncratic character have inspired countless attempts by Scots and outsiders alike to describe and define that mysterious Scottish essence. This present account will have achieved something if only to point out that there is much more to the heritage of Scotland than present perceptions seem to allow. In the popular imagination folkloric flourishes such as whisky, haggis, tartan and bagpipes loom large, as if these trappings on their own can sum up the identity of the country. This book is an attempt, albeit on a modest scale, to fill in some of the details of the amazingly rich and diverse historic reality which underlies the Scottish scene. Although this book can only scratch at the surface, it does aim to convey a comprehensive picture and to encourage a keener understanding of the heritage of Scotland which is still so vibrantly alive in the country's landscapes, buildings and ancient monuments. The book is structured in sections of photostories, each with a concise introduction. The result is of course a highly fragmented view of Scotland, but this is after all the way we perceive a physical reality.

Although today's image of Scotland has been largely obscured by the kilt-and-tartan mythology of the nineteenth century, this is at least one step better than the state of affairs around the middle of the eighteenth century, when even the name of Scotland had been dropped by the bureaucrats and was supplanted by the awful label of 'North Britain'. Thankfully the term has since disappeared, but the underlying notion of a territory of North Britain as a mere appendage to England has lingered on in the collective unconscious, denying the country of Scotland its essential differentness in terms of culture and heritage.

But even with the word 'Scotland' things are not as straightforward as they might seem, for the name was derived from just one of the several ethnic strains of the country's founding fathers. The Scots, a Celtic tribe of Irish origin, are relative newcomers as well; their 'Scottish' colony was established as recently as the fifth century AD. To the Scots themselves the country was known in their native Gaelic as Alba, so that if one were to look for an anglicised form of this original name then supposedly Scotland today might be another Albania. Curiously, the name given to the country by the Romans, Caledonia, has outlasted the Gaelic Alba and is often used today, especially in a poetic sense, to evoke the past glories of ancient Caledonia. Had the older population, known to us as the Picts, been able to withstand the takeover by the Scots, then we might be calling Scotland something like Pictavia.

Such conjectures are not entirely without point, for they underline the fact that Scotland is composed of an amalgam of peoples and races, by no means dominated by the Scots, whose name has been immortalised in the term Scotland. In addition to the Picts one must mention the Angles of Lothian and the Britons of Strathclyde as the

Tantallon Castle

indigenous inhabitants of Scotland at the dawn of history. The fifth strain to be added to the national bloodstock was Viking, especially strong in the territories of the northern and western seaboard. The Scots of today are descended from these original ethnic groups together with more recent additions.

This mixed parentage is particularly significant when one surveys the physical relics of the Scottish heritage, for these encompass a tremendous range of styles and inspiration. Yet for all the diversity there is also the germ of a native tradition which, although by no means unified, nevertheless stands apart from that of England. From the domestic structures of Neolithic Man right down to the houses of Charles Rennie Mackintosh there is a skilful and pleasing economy of means which is peculiarly Scottish. Nature, of course, has played an essential role in the shaping of Scottish building. Rugged mountains, a harsh climate and a progressive lack of trees have determined the predominance of stone for residences as diverse as the baronial tower-houses and the lowly black-houses. Lack of security in the land until as recently as the seventeenth century has endowed Scottish architecture with an added degree of defensive and watchful characteristics.

The highlights of Scottish building range from the great megalithic monuments of the third millennium BC and the enigmatic brochs of the Iron Age, the ultimate in defensive arrangements, to the glorious development of the tower-house in all its cunning variations throughout the Middle Ages. That so many of these tower-houses have survived until the present day, either as substantial ruins or virtually intact and still inhabited, is a testimonial to the craft of the builder-masons who also acted as architects. The tower-houses that still stud the landscape are a reminder also of the ancient powers of the clan chiefs and feudal barons who once held the people in subjection with the double threat of 'pit and gallows'.

Buildings of martial aspect thus bear witness to a turbulent past; but this was not always so. During Scotland's 'golden age' of the twelfth and thirteenth centuries there was a peaceful infiltration of Anglo-Norman influence and a veritable outpouring of wealth into the magnificent abbeys and cathedrals whose sad ruins are still immensely moving and impressive. These great buildings owed little to native architects but they do demonstrate that Scotland was in the mainstream of international, that is European, culture at that time. The endowment of the new collegiate churches in the fifteenth century marked a resurgence of a native style of ecclesiastical buildings which had lain dormant since the days of the old Celtic Church. Early Christian art in Scotland also owed much to the native genius of the Picts in particular, whose cross-slabs, symbol-stones and carved reliefs show a level of artistry unsurpassed by any subsequent achievements. The art of the Picts is probably the most unexpected chapter in the cultural history of Scotland.

Sadly there are few physical remains of a distinctively Norse character to show for the long Viking occupation of the Northern and Western Isles, except perhaps for the shape of the traditional Shetland boat and of the rectangular long-house, which replaced the local round or oval dwellings and became the standard type for the country as a whole. Likewise the Romans, those other invaders a few centuries earlier, have left little but military reminders of their troubled sojourn in Caledonia. However, the Antonine Wall has an ominous significance in that it prefigured a future border between the north and south of the island of Britain. But the Romans did not intermarry, which is in stark contrast to the Vikings whose blood proved to be such a potent addition to that of the Celtic clans.

The Celto-Norse aristocracy which emerged in the Hebrides was a proud, martial race who, as the Lords of the Isles, managed for centuries to steer an independent course between the competing claims of Norwegian, Scottish and English overlords. Much of the romance and poetry of Scotland is contained within the Lordship of the Isles, the last great flowering of the Gaelic-speaking peoples prior to their subjugation by the kings of Scotland who by the late Middle Ages were ethnically and culturally Anglo-Norman. The unrelenting suppression of the autonomous clans has been the leitmotif of Scottish history ever since the fifteenth century, a process leading from the forfeiture of the Lordship of the Isles, through the Massacre of Glencoe and the defeat of the Jacobite risings, and culminating in the Clearances, or mass evictions of Highland tenantry in the eighteenth and nineteenth centures. Thus the Scottish scene is pervaded by a sad absence: that of a vanished population. In the lonely glens there is a vast sense of the missing ones, long since departed overseas or to the tenements of Glasgow. Scotland is a land peopled by ghosts and memories. Much of Scottish legend is melancholic and nostalgic, a mood which accommodates such tragic destinies as that of Mary Queen of Scots and Bonny Prince Charlie.

Some aspects of the Scottish heritage tend to be overlooked because they do not fit easily into the national mould. The architectural genius of Robert Adam of Kirkcaldy is often viewed as an English phenomenon, which is hardly surprising since Adam took the road to London early in his career and most of his major buildings and interiors are to be found in England. However, such grand achievements as Edinburgh New Town, almost entirely conceived and executed by Scottish architects and planners, show that Scotland was more than a match for the senior partner in the union of the two countries. In proportion to its population Scotland probably produced more men of genius who made a vital contribution to the consolidation of the British Empire than did England itself. In this sense the Treaty of Union in 1707 brought about the end of a distinctively Scottish heritage, for the talent of the nation was henceforth to flower on a much broader stage. The export of Scottish ideas and brains has continued unabated to this day, and the national identity has become increasingly absorbed in the wider stream of contemporary developments. In order to appreciate the native genius of Scottish civilisation one must turn to the past and retrace the story from its distant origins.

1 The Shaping of the Landscape

In recent years there has been an immense advance in our knowledge of the distant origins of present landforms. This has been brought about by the science of plate tectonics, which postulates large-scale horizontal movements of the earth's rigid crust. As far as Scotland is concerned this has produced the finding that much of the material which constitutes the country today was first formed in the southern hemisphere. The story goes back at least 2,500 million years, during which not only were cataclysmic geological events reshaping the surface but the land itself was on the move, only arriving in its present northerly latitude as recently as 40 million years ago.

The oldest rocks to be found in Scotland are on the north-west of the mainland and the Outer Hebrides whose hard, grey, crystalline Lewisian gneiss was slowly formed from the melting and pressurising of volcanic ash and sand. By about 1,000 million years ago there had occurred an uplift of the Lewisian gneiss into a high plateau which has since been considerably eroded. Much of it is buried, however, beneath younger rocks known as the Moine series. The next major geological event was the formation of the Torridonian sandstone some 750 million years ago, a truly ancient rock which can be seen in the majestic peaks of Liathach and Beinn Eighe of the Torridon area; this is one of the most highly acclaimed landscapes in the Scottish Highlands, on account of its wild beauty.

Around 570 million years ago Scotland was still separated by an ocean basin from what was to become England and Wales. The geographical union of Scotland and England occurred at least 500 million years ago as this ocean subsided at a time when the combined land mass of the future British Isles still lay south of the equator. The thrusting, folding and uplift of the Highlands, which gave Scotland its characteristic faulting from the south-west to the north-east, also belongs to this period. By about 400 million years ago Scotland formed part of the great continent of Euramerica in the Old Red Sandstone period. The rugged cliffs of Hoy, and in particular the lofty 450-foot stack known as the Old Man of Hoy, are the dramatic relics of this chapter of Scotland's geological evolution.

By the beginning of the Carboniferous (or coal-producing) period 370 million years ago, Britain straddled the equator, and parts of Scotland were submerged in a warm, shallow sea. Intermittent eruptions of lava created, together with others, the volcanic hills of Edinburgh, notably Castle Rock itself. In Glasgow there is a striking reminder of this time in the Fossil Grove, which contains the petrified remains *in situ* of tree stumps some 330 million years old. These resemble no trees still in existence; their roots bifurcate from four main protuberances into eight equal branches, and then fork once more to create a total of sixteen branches on the ground from which a series of rootlets extended into the soft sand and mud. Such trees would have been at home in a tropical, swampy environment which is quite in accordance with the presumed equatorial position of Scotland at the time. It has been estimated that these trees grew to a height of 100 feet and that the weight of the structure was borne by the tubular strength of the tough outer layer of bark. Remains of similar trees have been discovered in the thick coal seams of the Glasgow region. This evidence of the type of vegetation from which coal was produced gives the Fossil Grove a direct relevance to Glasgow's subsequent industrial development which was powered by coal. The miraculous survival of this natural graveyard of ancient trees was due to the accidents of faulting, uplift and folding of the rock which brought the Fossil Grove to the surface but protected it from erosion with an overlying sheet of hard, igneous rock. Thus by chance this most impressive group of fossil trees in Britain was eventually discovered as recently as 1887.

As the land mass bearing Scotland and England moved slowly north between 280 and 135 million years ago, it experienced a hot, arid climate, which was the environment encountered by the dinosaurs some 200 million years ago. Glasgow's Hunterian Museum contains the first well-documented example in Scotland of a dinosaur's footprint. It is preserved in a block of limestone discovered in 1982 below the cliffs south of Rubha nam Braithairean by Trotternish on Skye. The footprint is 170 million years old and belongs to the Middle Jurassic period.

Some of Scotland's most spectacular rock formations date back to a time of intense volcanic activity which commenced 58 million years ago, after the Atlantic Ocean had been formed. The Western Highlands and Islands contain the finest examples of these, the youngest of Scotland's hard rocks. The towers and spires of the Quirang in north Skye are a truly wondrous sight as might appear in an artist's impression of a fantasy landscape. The hexagonal columns of black basalt of Fingal's Cave on the island of Staffa are the result of the curious effects of the cooling lava which had burst through at many locations along what is now the western seaboard of Scotland. The Burg on the Isle of Mull has affinities with Staffa; its strange rock formation, known as McCulloch's Tree, is about 50 million years old.

The mountains of the Scottish Highlands were once as high as are the Himalayas in our day, but rapid and extensive erosion during the Tertiary Period, 10 to 1.5 million years ago, has substantially reduced them. It is estimated that Rhum and Skye lost 1,000 metres of rock and Arran as much as 2,500 metres during this time. Ben Nevis, Scotland's highest peak, is now a mere 1,344 metres. However, despite their relatively low altitudes, Scotland's mountains continue to impress on account of their stark appearance and abrupt rise from sea level to pre-alpine conditions. Eroded as they are, the Scottish Highlands stand apart from the rest of the country, their backs turned to the Lowlands of the south-east and their arms extended far out into the Atlantic. This outward-looking mountain fastness of the Highlands came to determine the cultural and historical development of the region as a distinct entity. Even the greatest of the fault lines – the Great Glen running from Fort William to Inverness via Loch Linnhe, Loch Lochy and Loch Ness – does not permit access to the Highlands but merely provides a convenient corridor for passing from the Atlantic to the North Sea, a possibility at last realised by the Caledonian Canal in the nineteenth century.

The final great natural occurrence in the shaping of the Scottish landscape was the

Fossil Grove, Victoria Park, Glasgow

glaciation during the succession of ice ages which lasted some 2.5 million years. The effects of glaciation were diverse, according to the region and the nature of the ice cover. The western part of the country bears the most obvious scars with the characteristic smooth U-shaped valleys scoured out by the glaciers, corries, screes of frost-shattered rock, glacial deposits in the shape of drumlins, and even the preserved strandlines of a series of ice-dammed lakes known as the 'parallel roads' of Glen Roy. In the Outer Hebrides there are some remarkable examples of a flat ice-sculptured landscape of the 'knock and lochan' type (hill and little loch). Parts of North Uist were scoured by glaciation into a wilderness which now consists more of water than land. Of all the natural phenomena which gave Scotland its present appearance none is more noticeable in effect than glaciation.

As the ice finally receded from Scotland as recently as 10,000 BC so the land released from the great weight of the ice rose in relation to the seas which also swelled from the meltwater. This lifting of the land mass led to the formation of raised beaches from 50 to 100 feet above sea level; the Old Course at St Andrews is on a typical raised beach. These platforms of land by the sea have an archaeological significance for they contain some of the earliest sites of human occupation from the Mesolithic (Middle Stone Age) which extended from 7000 BC to 4000 BC. These sites probably represent the earliest presence of humans in Scotland, for it is improbable that Palaeolithic (Old Stone Age) Man would have found even a toehold on which to base an existence during the Ice Age in Scotland. Any surface evidence of Palaeolithic occupation during an interglacial period would, however, have been erased during the ensuing glaciation.

With the improvement of the climate following the Ice Age the post-glacial terrain would have evolved firstly as a tundra of open grasslands offering scope for the hunting of herds of reindeer. Then with a further warming there was an extension northwards of tree cover, notably birch, rowan and Scots pine in the north and upland locations and oak, ash and elm in the south and more sheltered localities of the north and west. This thick cover of primaeval forest reached its maximum extent at an altitude some 300 metres above its present level. The treelessness of vast tracts of the Highlands today is partly due to man's despoiling activities, but also to a marked deterioration of the climate which began in the second millennium BC and which is still with us. It is now extremely difficult to find examples of native woodland. There are only isolated stands of oak, but the Scots pine is more in evidence, notably in the magnificent forest at Rothiemurchus.

However, it was a densely wooded country that was encountered by the Mesolithic peoples who moved into Scotland, or rather skirted its shores, from about 7000 BC. The Mesolithic way of life was essentially the nomadic pattern of the hunter-gatherer, following seasonal supplies of fish and crustaceans and the game such as red deer which abounded in the forests. No traces of any permanent Mesolithic dwelling have been found in Scotland, and the remains of these people are mainly of the 'campsite' variety, such as by the river Lussa on Jura, where a 'hearth' of three abutting stone rings from about 6000 BC has been discovered. The other Mesolithic remains are the 'middens' or heaps of refuse, consisting mainly of shellfish, such as the remarkable mounds on Oronsay which go back to the middle of the fifth millennium BC. Knowledge of Mesolithic occupation in Scotland can now be extended as far back as the middle of the seventh millennium BC. Carbon dating of hazelnuts excavated at Farm Fields by Kinloch on the Isle of Rhum in 1984, which were found together with a collection of flaked lithic material including a core of local bloodstone, from which several blades had been struck, puts the earliest known site of human occupation in Scotland between 6575 and 6531 BC.

Although the Neolithic (New Stone Age) settlers are credited with the introduction of farming to Scotland from about 4000 BC there is some evidence that the first attempts at forest clearance may go back to just before 5000 BC. With the exception of some recent efforts, deforestation has been the sad and remorseless leitmotif of man's contribution to the natural landscape ever since. This increasing lack of trees reached its worst in the eighteenth century when Dr Johnson remarked that, 'A tree might be a show in

Ice Age landscape near Ben Buie, Mull

Scotland as a horse in Venice'. The possibility of so barren a landscape would have been way beyond the comprehension of the Mesolithic and Neolithic inhabitants of Scotland who were confronted by an impenetrable wall of forest. Such was the natural stage which successive generations were to subdue and almost eradicate in the process of establishing human civilisation in the wilds of Scotland.

GAZETTEER 1

National Nature Reserves
1 Beinn Eighe
2 Ben Lawers (NTS)
3 Caerlaverock
4 Cairngorms
5 Corrieshalloch (NTS)
6 Craigellachie
7 Glen Roy
8 Glen Tanar
9 Inverpolly
10 Loch Druidibeg
11 Loch Lomond
12 Noss
13 Rhum
14 St Kilda (NTS)

Natural Features
15 Ailsa Craig
16 Bass Rock
17 Bullers of Buchanan
18 Carsaig Arches
19 Devil's Beef Tub
20 Devil's Mill and Cauldron Linn
21 Eas Coul Aulin
22 Falls of Glomach
23 Falls of Shin
24 Fingal's Cave
25 Fossil Grove
26 Grey Mare's Tail (NTS)
27 Kilt Rock
28 North Berwick Law
29 Old Man of Hoy
30 Old Man of Storr (see Storr)
31 Parallel Roads of Glen Roy (see Glen Roy)

32 Quirang
33 Randolph's Leap
34 Smoo Cave
35 Whiten Head

Other Areas of Scenic and Wildlife Interest
36 Argyll Forest Park
37 Balranald Nature Reserve
38 The Burg (NTS)
39 Cairngorm Pine Forest Centre
40 Fair Isle (NTS)
41 Farigaig Forest Centre
42 Fowlsheugh Nature Reserve (RSPB)
43 Galloway Forest Park
44 Glencoe and Dalness (NTS)
45 Glengoulandie Deer Park
46 Glenmore Forest Park
47 Goatfell (NTS)
48 Handa Island Nature Reserve (RSPB)
49 Highland Wildlife Park
50 Kintail (NTS)
51 Loch an Eilean Visitor Centre
52 Lochwinnoch Nature Reserve (RSPB)
53 Storr
54 Torridon (NTS)

Note
NTS – National Trust for Scotland
RSPB – Royal Society for the Protection of Birds
The National Nature Reserves listed above are a selection of the areas in Scotland designated as NNRs by the Nature Conservancy Council.

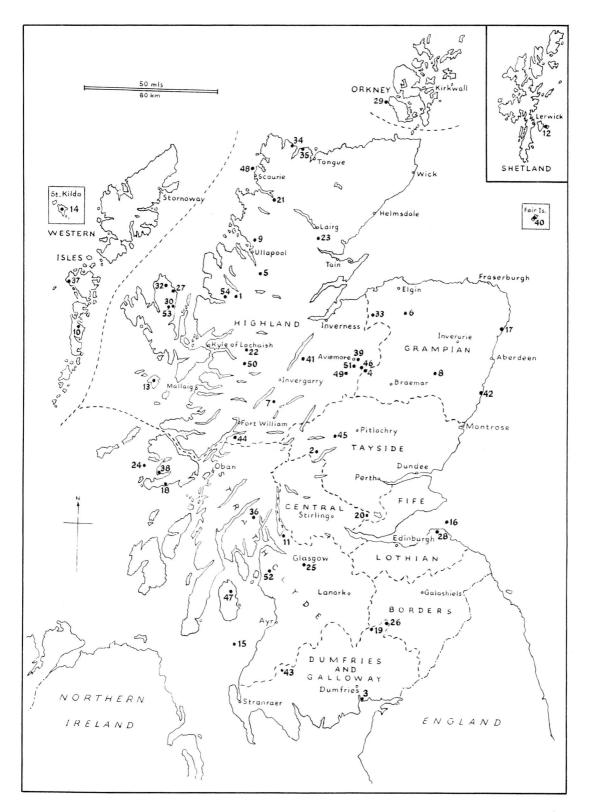

50 mls
80 km

ORKNEY
Kirkwall
29

SHETLAND
Lerwick
12

Fair Is.
40

St.Kilda
14
WESTERN
ISLES

Stornoway

34
35 Tongue
48 Scourie
21
Wick
Helmsdale
Lairg
9
Ullapool
23
Tain
5

37

32 27
30
53

54 1

HIGHLAND

Inverness

Elgin
33
6

Fraserburgh

Inverurie
GRAMPIAN
17
Aberdeen

10

Kyle of Lochaish
22
50

41 Aviemore
51 46
49 4
39
8

Braemar
42

13 Mallaig

7

Fort William
44

Invergarry

Pitlochry

Montrose

2
45
TAYSIDE
Dundee

24 38
18

Oban

Perth

36
CENTRAL
Stirling

20

FIFE

11

Glasgow
25

52

47

Lanark

Edinburgh
16
28
LOTHIAN

Galashiels

BORDERS
26
19

Ayr

15

43

DUMFRIES
AND
GALLOWAY
Dumfries 3

Stranraer

NORTHERN
IRELAND

ENGLAND

N

19

2 Landmarks of Prehistory

Those who look to the Middle East for the very beginnings of man's march along the road of civilisation have tended to view human progress, at least in the early stages, as emanating exclusively from that region and spreading slowly like the ripples on a pond which gradually weaken as they reach the areas on the periphery. According to this 'diffusionist' theory it would be expected that Scotland would simply provide a belated, provincial reflection of foreign culture. In fact, quite to the contrary, Scotland's Neolithic or New Stone Age makes a grand and confident entry in the architectural annals with some splendid megalithic works of sophisticated design and engineering. Here on the extreme north-west fringe of Europe is the early third millennium BC masterpiece of Maes Howe, a finely constructed chambered tomb which predates the pyramids of the Nile Valley. The remains of domestic architecture on Orkney take us even further back in time with the settlement of Skara Brae already in occupation around 3100 BC and the houses at Knap of Howar as early as 3500 BC. Such a timescale calls for further study of the spread of building technology in European prehistory, for the simple notion of all knowledge coming exclusively from the lands of the east would appear no longer tenable. Even within the British context it would appear that the north was at one time ahead of the south, for the Ring of Brodgar on Orkney and the Callanish Standing Stones on Lewis are more ancient than the great stone circles of Avebury and Stonehenge.

A considerable controversy has been stirred up by the supposed scientific knowledge of the Neolithic folk who constructed Callanish and the Ring of Brodgar and other stone settings with astronomical points of reference. Although the new school of archaeo-astronomy often goes too far in its claims for such sites and generally assumes a highly advanced mathematical knowledge, for which no other evidence exists, conventional wisdom shows too patronising a view of the intellectual capacities of our ancestors. It should be borne in mind that what the people of the third millennium BC lacked in terms of precise astronomical knowledge was probably compensated in part by a keener and more intimate awareness of the movements of the heavenly bodies. It may thus be safely concluded that the alignments of such monuments as Callanish and the Ring of Brodgar are clearly related to sightings of the moon and the stars, without amounting to what could be called accurate observatories by the standards of the twentieth century.

It may appear strange that the flourishing centres of Neolithic civilisation in Scotland are mainly remote in terms of today's spread of population, occurring in the marginal areas of the Western and Northern Isles. However, the mainland at that time was still heavily wooded up to at least 1,000 feet, and this, together with the mountainous terrain, must have posed a formidable obstacle to the forms of land transport then

Cullerlie Stone Circle

available. Communications by water must therefore have been of overwhelming importance to the early settlers, so that the islands of Scotland were not in reality isolated by the sea but linked to one another by maritime connections. Even today there are places on the western coast of the Scottish mainland, notably near Cape Wrath and in Knoydart, where the inhabitants must take a ferry even to reach other parts of the mainland. In Neolithic times the interior of the Highlands was almost impenetrable and untouched by man save for the Great Glen, which offered a convenient short-cut between the east and west with long stretches of loch and only brief overland crossings. Water transport has always been of prime significance in Scotland's development.

No complex navigational skills need be supposed, for it was possible to sail as far north as Shetland without losing sight of the land, but even progress by strand-looping in those unpredictable waters must have required a high degree of seamanship as well as sturdy vessels. Whilst the evidence provided by archaeology has defined the Neolithic peoples as peasant-farmers, nothing has been discovered to cast light on their undoubted prowess as seafarers. Whatever was the nature of their boats – either superior coracle-type or dug-out – it is clear that the crossing of the waters did not daunt Scotland's Neolithic founding fathers who sought out the tiniest and remotest of islands for their settlements and simple homesteads.

The attractions of Orkney may well have included the relative treelessness of the environment. This would have been quite an incentive to immigration for those faced with the alternative prospect of clearing virgin forest on the mainland with the stone axes available at the time. Perhaps there was also mounting pressure for good land further south which drove settlers to Orkney, but the islands, once inhabited, soon developed into one of the great cultural centres of Neolithic civilisation in Europe. Maes Howe, the Ring of Brodgar and Skara Brae are but the three most illustrious sites on Orkney which bear witness to the extensive occupation of the islands in the period between the fourth and second millennia BC.

Orkney in the twentieth century AD is still good farming country, but this does not apply to some of the other areas settled by the Neolithic farmers. In the Outer Hebrides in particular, the places which once supported a large number of scattered communities around four to five thousand years ago now consist of marginally productive land or peat bogs. This is a direct result of the overall deterioration in the climate which set in about 1500 BC and was especially dire in northern and western regions. The colder, wetter weather inexorably wrought dramatic changes in the landscape, denuding the higher slopes of their forest cover, leaching the soil of its nutritive elements and encouraging the formation of peat. Perhaps it was the worsening climate and its after-effects which caused what appears to have been a cultural eclipse in the Northern and Western Isles by the end of the Bronze Age. A measure of the importance of the Outer Hebrides during the Early Bronze Age, roughly between 2000 and 1500 BC, may be gauged on the island of Lewis where, in addition to the Callanish Standing Stones, the remains of twenty-one other stone circles have been discovered. It is probable that further evidence of a flourishing Bronze Age culture is available in ample measure on Lewis buried at least five feet beneath the peat which has accumulated there in the meantime.

The transition from the Neolithic or New Stone Age to the Bronze Age and then to the Iron Age is a somewhat elusive process to define, for the respective cultures are described purely in terms of their tool-making technology. At one unique site it is possible to obtain a glimpse of prehistory in the making in terms of architecture: Jarlshof on Shetland presents a succession of settlements which straddle the Stone Age to the Iron Age, and indeed take us far beyond that through to the Middle Ages and the seventeenth century of our own era.

Jarlshof's fascinating record of human occupation commences with a group of oval stone huts which date from around the middle of the second millennium BC until the middle of the first millennium BC. These have thick stone walls as well as piers which provide subdivisions of the internal space. Here, around 600 BC in what was still a Stone Age community there appeared on the scene a bronzesmith practising the new technology. Remnants from his workshop, installed in one of the houses, include a number of clay moulds for bronze axe heads, sword blades and ornaments. Thanks to a dagger of recognisable Irish pattern found at the site, the bronzesmith has been identified as a migrant worker from Ireland. He thus becomes one of the first anonymous personalities – along with the lady who dropped her beads during the evacuation of Skara Brae in 2450 BC – to enter the stage of Scottish prehistory.

The Iron Age at Jarlshof is witnessed by a group of houses from the very end of the first millennium BC which are divided into radial segments. These were followed by the construction of a broch, that mysterious and typically Scottish circular tower of defence. The foundation of the broch has been shown to be resting on a layer of wind-blown sand, a sure indication that the site had previously been abandoned for a while. An aisled round-house was later built within the enclosure surrounding the broch, and quite probably stone from the broch was used in the process. Further demolition was caused by the subsequent construction of two wheel-houses in around AD 500. The evolution of Jarlshof extends into the Middle Ages with some characteristic long-houses of the Vikings, and the latest structure on the site is relatively modern, a house of substantial size built about 1600.

The archaeological complex at Jarlshof is a fine illustration of the process by which one layer of civilisation comes to supplant that preceding it, often recycling the building materials at hand. But Jarlshof also demonstrates that the chronology of prehistory is no exact science, for in reality the introduction of the new technologies occurred at different times in different places, and here was a Stone Age culture which survived well into the period classified as the Bronze Age, and indeed almost into the Iron Age as well. It would appear then that Shetland was rather lagging behind for a while before joining the mainstream of technology.

Albeit with such regional variations, there was a marked migration into Scotland of a bronze-using people from around 2000 BC and their presence did more than introduce a new metal technology. The Beaker Folk, as they are called from their custom of placing a pottery urn with their burials, began a radically novel method of interment, individual rather than collective. What this meant in terms of philosophy and religious outlook is impossible to say, but it is perhaps significant that the salvation of the individual was to be the main thrust of subsequent religious development. This meeting of Bronze Age and Stone Age burial customs and their associated architecture can be witnessed at the

Cairnpapple Hill

hill called Cairnpapple, situated about eighteen miles to the west of Edinburgh. Here there are burials of the Beaker Folk within a henge going back to the Neolithic Age. There was a dramatic transformation of the site between 2000 and 1600 BC when a new, larger cairn engulfed the earlier structure and the stone circle was demolished in order to provide kerbstones for the extended cairn. Altogether, it has been shown that Cairnpapple was in use as a sacred site and burial place for as long as 3,000 years.

The Iron Age Celts, who moved into Scotland from at least the seventh century BC, introduced several new forms of settlement. At first they favoured single steadings and isolated farms, but in the closing centuries of the first millennium BC there was a phenomenal growth in the number of defensive structures which clearly reflect worsening conditions of security. A fresh influx of Celtic warrior aristocracies which subjugated the local populations is a possible explanation for the tremendous development of hilltop fortifications from which the tribal chieftains vied with one another for the most obvious form of territorial control, the mastery of the strategic heights. In the first centuries AD there was additional cause for alarm on account of the advance of the Romans, but the external threat was apparently not enough to bring about a lasting and effective union of the Celtic tribes. Tacitus wrote of them, 'Fortune can give us no greater boon than discord among our foes', and there is every sign that the tribal leaders feared more attacks from their rival counterparts than from the Romans. Clan warfare – a recurrent theme of subsequent Scottish history – may be said to begin here.

The builders of the hillforts were Celtic tribes such as the Selgovae at Eildon Hill North and the Votadini at Traprain Law. A study of the hillforts of south-east Scotland is particularly instructive for the light they shed on the details of the Roman advance during the first centuries AD. Both at Eildon Hill North and at Woden Law there are clear signs of the Romans supplanting the Celtic tribes as the masters of the hilltops. These Iron Age Celts whom the Romans encountered were linguistically of the P-Celtic, or Gallo-Brittonic branch, to which the Welsh and the Bretons also belong. The Q-Celtic, or Gaelic-speaking Celts did not enter Scotland until the fifth century AD from Ireland. There are also traces of a previous non-Celtic language in Scotland, which has survived in certain place-names, but it is extremely unlikely that we shall ever gain any knowledge of the languages spoken in Scotland prior to the arrival of the Celts.

In addition to the hillforts there are a number of other characteristic structures to be found in Scotland at the time of the Roman offensive, and they all bear the unmistakable marks of those unsettled times with an overriding concern for security. An instinct for defence at all costs is the common feature of a number of otherwise disparate forms of habitation such as the broch, the dun, the crannog, and the earth-house. Each is a fine example of small-scale defensive tactics combined with a spartan domesticity. The circular stone tower of the broch is the most resolutely Scottish architectural structure. There are hundreds of examples mainly in the north and west in the areas which were to remain outside the Roman theatre of action, and it is possible that the distribution of broch sites in Scotland may be an indication of a people or group of peoples quite distinct from the inhabitants of the hillforts in the south-east. The dun was also a structure of stone but more in the form of a defensive wall than a tower. There are large duns protecting the summit of a hill and much smaller versions which are roughly equivalent to a defensive farmstead. The crannog was a timber stronghold

Ring of Brodgar, Orkney

built on an artificial island of logs set in a lake. Access to the crannog was usually by a causeway, concealed just beneath the surface of the water so that any intruders would have to pick their way carefully and thus lose the element of surprise of a rushed assault. The earth-house, known also as 'souterrain' or as 'weem', is a curious phenomenon consisting of a curved subterranean passage between a group of huts which seems to have served as a form of emergency storage or hide-out. Such were the types of residence in favour with the peoples of Scotland in the first centuries AD as the mists of prehistoric times were slowly lifting to allow the occasional and elusive glimpse of actual events, such as the Roman victory at Mons Graupius in AD 84, and of real personalities, such as the defeated Celtic leader on that occasion, known as Calgacus.

When passed in quick review the 3,000 years of Scottish prehistory from the third millennium until the advance of the Romans show a dramatic reversal of the country's position. In addition to the marked deterioration of the climate since Neolithic times there had also been a change in the cultural position. The great works of the Neolithic peoples in Scotland such as Maes Howe, Callanish and the Ring of Brodgar were outstanding examples of architectural achievement around the third millennium BC, but by the first millennium BC Scotland's position may be described as marginal in terms of the civilisation of the day which was developing in the lands of the east. Seen in retrospect, the Neolithic period of Scotland appears to stand out as a more distant golden age with its sunnier clime and great works of collective genius which still impress us today.

Chambered Tombs

At a distance the mysteriously named Grey Cairns of Camster form a curious element in the bleak landscape of Caithness: just a long, low outline rising above the moor suggesting the back of a partially submerged whale. On closer inspection the main cairn reveals two low entrances in the mound of stones which lead via short passages into two separate chambers, of surprisingly small dimensions by comparison with the overall scale of the cairn, which with its four horns occupies a space measuring 200 by 65 feet.

Just 200 yards away is a second, circular cairn where remains of cremations, rudimentary artefacts and Neolithic pottery have been discovered. Today the Grey Cairns of Camster are remote from any human settlement and stand surrounded by a vast expanse of peat bog, but during the Neolithic Age with its drier, sunnier climate the land hereabouts must have supported a sizeable farming community which built these

impressive monuments for its dead.

Further north, over the waters of the Pentland Firth on the islands of Orkney, is the most intriguing collection of prehistoric chambered tombs in the whole of Britain. Such is the concentration of ancient funerary monuments in Orkney that one is liable to think of the islands as a sort of Neolithic necropolis, but the rich agriculture attracted settlement from the south from the earliest times. If the evidence of their tombs is any indication, then the Orcadians of 5,000 years ago must have been in the vanguard of Neolithic technology. The chambered tomb of Maes Howe is recognised as the supreme example of design and engineering of the prehistoric peoples of Scotland, perhaps of Europe. Its central chamber is 15-foot square and its walls support a corbelled vault almost

Maes Howe, Orkney

Grey Cairns of Camster

18 feet above the ground. In contrast to most burial chambers Maes Howe shows a remarkable degree of symmetry and precision. With the exception of the wall which contains the entrance passage, there is a cell giving off on each side of the square. The drystone masonry is so tightly fitted together that the blade of a knife cannot be inserted between the courses.

Maes Howe was first properly excavated in 1861 but several parties of Norsemen had previously broken into the tomb and taken whatever of value it might have contained. One group of Norsemen in the twelfth century took the trouble to carve some fine runic inscriptions with tantalising references to a great treasure which had been carried away. But the most exciting feature of Maes Howe is the alignment of the entrance passage, which allows the rays of the sun to penetrate the gloom of the inner chamber only on one day a year, at midwinter precisely. This phenomenon not only presupposes a certain skill in astronomical observation but also suggests a clue to the ritual and mythology of Neolithic Orcadians, for whom the turning point of the long, dark winter would naturally be an event of the greatest significance. But the most noteworthy fact about Maes Howe for archaeologists and historians is the extremely early dating of the site; radiocarbon analysis of peat samples from the surrounding ditch indicates that the cairn was built before 2700 BC, thus predating the pyramids of Egypt's Old Kingdom.

Also on Orkney, the chambered tomb of Quanterness which goes back to the fourth

29

Clava Cairns

millennium BC, and that of Quoyness on the smaller island of Sanday which was in use by about 2900 BC, reinforce the picture of a thriving and advanced community in this part of the Northern Isles some five thousand years ago. The tiny island of Rousay just off the mainland of Orkney today supports a mere 250 inhabitants; but it is a veritable museum of prehistoric burial practices with a string of chambered tombs such as Midhowe, Knowe of Yarso, Blackhammer and Taversoe Tuick. The excavations at Midhowe revealed a 78-foot gallery-style chamber, divided into twelve separate stalls along each side. The list of ancient tombs on Orkney shows a great diversity in style and layout and amounts to a considerable inventory, but there is none more curious than the Dwarfie Stane on the island of Hoy, a unique specimen where the burial chamber has been carved from a single block of sandstone.

Neolithic Man is thought to have made his way to the Northern Isles of Scotland in a series of short sea voyages via Ireland, Argyll and the Western Isles, taking the short cut through the Great Glen in preference to the hazardous sail around Cape Wrath. Confirmation of this theory may be seen in the

Maes Howe, Orkney – inside the burial chamber

distribution of ancient graves throughout Argyll, Arran, Bute and the Hebrides, with a cluster of cairns at the northern end of the Great Glen, where the Clava Cairns form part of what appears to be an elongated necropolis with eight cairns along a three-quarter-mile stretch of the River Nairn.

Although the architectural details of Scotland's chambered tombs have been subjected to the most painstaking analysis, there is nothing that tells of the beliefs of the people who built them or of their vision of the afterlife. However, it does seem that burial sites did occupy a prominent place in the lives of the living communities. It has also been stressed that the communal nature of the tombs indicates an egalitarian society, at least in respect of the afterlife. There appears to be no class distinction between kings or chieftains and the ordinary mass of folk. But the greatest mystery still surrounding Scotland's prehistoric tombs is on account

Dwarfie Stane, Hoy

of their extremely early chronology. For it leaves us at a loss to explain the precise origins of this vigorous Neolithic culture on the north-west frontier of Europe.

Ring of Brodgar – an enduring symbol of Neolithic culture

The Riddle of the Stones

Unlike the chambered tombs which might be part of a broader European tradition, there is another class of megalithic monuments comprising stone circles and henges, unique to the British Isles, of which Scotland possesses the finest examples in the Ring of Brodgar on Orkney and the Callanish Standing Stones on Lewis.

The Ring of Brodgar, classified as a 'henge' on account of the ditch which surrounds the almost circular ring of stones, occupies a most dramatic setting on a narrow strip of land between the waters of Loch of Stenness and Loch of Harray. It has been calculated that the rock-cut ditch may have required as many as 80,000 man-hours of work, a finding which would argue strongly for a high degree of communal effort as well as a sizeable population. Originally there were 66 standing stones in the circle but only 36 survive, either as truncated stumps or fairly intact.

Research undertaken by Professor Alexander Thom claims that an ancient measure, the 'megalithic yard' corresponding to 2.72 feet, was the standard linear unit employed in the design. An underlying mathematical precision has been identified by some to indicate a clear astronomical function, but opinion is sharply divided as to the actual efficiency of such an early 'observatory'. Whatever the truth of the

matter, there is no escaping the powerful magic of the spot with its grand interplay of the elemental forces of earth, sky and water; and there seems little doubt of a potential ritualistic purpose with some relation to the movements of the moon and the stars.

Just under a mile away are the Stones of Stenness, a slightly earlier site dating back to the early third millennium BC, of which but a handful of the original twelve stones remain. From here, as from the Ring of Brodgar, there are distant views of the cliffs of the island of Hoy. Both stone circles are within sight of Maes Howe and of many places in the locality, a fact which suggests their central rôle in the lives of the communities scattered round about.

If the Ring of Brodgar may be likened to a vast arena with a circle of stones as its circumference, then the Callanish Standing Stones represent a very different use of space. The stones, of which 53 remain, are

Loanhead Stone Circle near Daviot

set on a slight ridge overlooking the open Atlantic. They form a tight inner circle from which emanate three short rows and one long double row of stones, a configuration which has reminded some observers of the shape of a Celtic cross. Whereas the Ring of Brodgar seems to invite a mighty throng for a ritualistic gathering, the stones of Callanish, almost huddled together at the centre and converging on a great monolith sixteen feet high, appear to be engaged in a secret meeting of their own, each stone with its weird natural features suggesting an individual character.

The dating of Callanish is extremely difficult, with the proposed span of construction extending from 3000 BC to 1500 BC. The stones do not stand in what would have been their original natural surrounding for some five feet of peat had accumulated on the site before peat cutting commenced at the end of the eighteenth century. A proper excavation was undertaken in 1857 by the owner of Lewis, Sir James Matheson, but even before this, theories and fantasies of considerable ingenuity had been woven around the origins and significance of the stones. These included the notion of a druidic temple, of a magic place for fertility rites with the monolith as

the phallus, and even of a Christian use of the site.

There was also the idea that Callanish served as a primitive lunar observatory, a possibility that has been seriously investigated in recent years. A new school of archaeo-astronomers has sought to prove that the latitude and alignment of the Callanish stones were precisely chosen in order to observe the phenomenon of the 'moon skim' which occurs at this site at exact intervals of 18.61 years. Although such ideas have been met with much scepticism by traditional archaeologists, it can easily be imagined why such lunar observations would be of use to a farming community as a means of establishing a basic calendar for the sewing of crops and other events of the agricultural year.

The spectacular stone circles of Brodgar and Callanish should not be seen in isolation, for they were part of a broader spread of similar megalithic structures and they rank as the supreme achievements among a great number of more modest monuments. As far afield as Arran, Mull, Argyll and Aberdeen-shire there was a firm tradition of building stone circles from early in the third millennium BC until the middle of the second millennium BC. The Scottish stone circles

have much in common with Irish monuments as well as with the great stone circles of Wessex at Stonehenge and Avebury. Callanish and the Ring of Brodgar were not, however, mere tributaries or outliers of the southern tradition. In fact there is every likelihood that the cultural transference worked in the opposite direction from north to south, for the Ring of Brodgar was built centuries before Avebury and Stonehenge, which might well represent the final flowering of ideas which began on Orkney.

Whatever proof may be lacking to establish such a connection beyond doubt, there is no

Callanish Standing Stones, Isle of Lewis

escaping the conclusion that the periphery of the British Isles, notably Orkney and the Hebrides, consisted during the Neolithic and Bronze Ages not of isolated and backward communities but of vigorously creative cultural centres in their own right which had the capability to transmit as well as to receive ideas. In reality the sea did not so much isolate the peoples of the Western and Northern Isles of Scotland as provide them with an open highway for communication in all directions.

Neolithic Domesticity

The almost total lack of remains of the dwellings of the people who built the great megalithic monuments in Scotland is generally explained by the fact that the construction materials such as wood were of an extremely perishable nature. The exception to the rule is to be found on Orkney where an entire Neolithic settlement with walls still standing up to eaves level has been wondrously preserved by an accident of nature at the place known as Skara Brae. That these houses of more than five thousand years ago have survived almost intact is indirectly due to the treeless environment of Orkney which obliged the first settlers to use durable

stone for even the humblest of structures. Equally important in the preservation of Skara Brae was the protective layer of sand which covered the site until recent times.

The re-emergence of Skara Brae from its sandy grave occurred in the wake of a violent storm around 1850 which partially exposed the stone houses. Since then six excavation campaigns have been conducted to reveal fully the extent of the occupation of the site from as early as 3100 BC until 2450 BC. During this time the population reached an average level of about thirty persons living in a tight huddle of up to eight one-room houses. Since much of the furniture was also of stone it has survived to allow an amazingly intimate reconstruction of the daily routine of the inhabitants. Exposed to view are the built-in stone dressers, central hearths and

Skara Brae, Orkney – house interior

even clay-lined storage tanks; box-like beds, not unlike those still in use in crofters' homes well into the twentieth century, were probably the only private spaces in what must have been intensely communal homes.

Evidence taken from the kitchen middens points to some limited cultivation of grain to supplement the basic diet of wild and domesticated animals and marine shellfish, notably limpets, which might have been kept fresh in the storage tanks sunk into the floors of the houses. Implements were fashioned from bone, both from birds and land animals as well as from the occasional beached whale left stranded by the sea. Whatever timber was used to support the roofs doubtless came in the form of driftwood from the ocean as well.

What makes Skara Brae such an exciting phenomenon is that it represents a freeze-frame picture of Neolithic domesticity with

no overlay of Bronze or Iron Age occupation. For, at some time around 2450 BC a gale, similar to the one that exposed the site in 1850, buried the settlement in a sand drift with such speed that the inhabitants had barely enough time to evacuate their homes. The beads of a necklace scattered at random along one of the 'streets' of Skara Brae tell of a desperate rush to safety which left no time to gather up precious possessions. And so Skara Brae was doomed to lie beneath the sand for about four and a half thousand years, like a more ancient Orcadian version of Pompeii, awaiting eventual rediscovery by a remote generation of humans.

The ruins have now been signposted and presented for view in a vivid way but it still requires a great effort of the imagination to picture the reality of everyday life in Skara Brae. We have to see the close-knit group of dwellings with their twisting passages serving

Skara Brae, Orkney – a settlement of the New Stone Age

as streets not exposed to the sky but covered over with circular roofs and buried under their own refuse. Down below would have been a world of permanent semi-darkness, an atmosphere filled with smoke and the pungent aromas of a confined habitation without proper sanitation.

It was the gradual process of coastal erosion which revealed another remarkable site of Neolithic occupation on the tiny Orkney island of Papa Westray. The small homestead of Knap of Howar, which was excavated in the 1930s, consists of two interconnecting homes – perhaps a pair of Neolithic semi-detached. These rectilinear structures with rounded ends have been dated by radiocarbon analysis of food debris back as early as 3500 BC, thus qualifying the Knap of Howar as the oldest known domestic housing in northern Europe. The presence of Unstan pottery, named after the chambered tomb on Orkney where the first sherds of that type were found, shows that Knap of Howar was occupied by people of the same culture as the tomb builders. The houses are now located directly by the beach but originally they were set well back from the sea. Like Skara Brae this settlement was also buried beneath an enormous sand drift which ensured its preservation from about 3100 BC until the twentieth century.

The temptation to generalise about Neolithic housing from the evidence of Skara Brae and Knap of Howar is to be cautiously resisted since even Shetland, with a roughly comparable situation, presents a remarkably different picture. Here only isolated examples of oval-shaped houses have been discovered, and the enigmatic 'temple' at Stanydale which is without parallel elsewhere. Nevertheless, some of the Neolithic building techniques, such as the

Knap of Howar, Papa Westray

drystone cavity walling, were still practised in the Northern and Western Isles of Scotland until the importation of bricks and breeze blocks in our own times. It is quite possible that there are further examples of the Skara Brae type to be uncovered on Orkney. A settlement of similar size, antiquity and state of preservation has been excavated on the tiny island of Rousay, but the site of Rinyo, as it is called, has been buried again and it now lies concealed beneath the green fields of a farm. The evidence of Rinyo, Knap of Howar, and Skara Brae points in the same direction as that provided by the chambered tombs and stone circles: namely that Orkney around five thousand years ago was not a last outpost of Neolithic civilisation but an advanced creative centre in its own right and well placed to enjoy the maritime traffic of that time. The joint advantages of Orkney's good farming land and strategic sea communications were to be even more fully exploited in the Middle Ages by the Norsemen who came to occupy the islands.

Knap of Howar, Papa Westray – house interior

The Brochs – A Scottish Enigma

Scotland possesses some five hundred of these mysterious round structures, which in terms of today's architectural forms are usually likened to a smaller version of the cooling tower at a modern power station.

Little is known of the origins of the broch, but it is regarded as a purely Scottish phenomenon which evolved around the first century BC. A map of broch distribution shows that they are for the most part clustered in thick concentrations in Skye, Caithness, Sutherland and the Northern Isles.

A rapid tour of the most spectacular and complete of the brochs, that of Mousa on

Dun Telve, Glenelg – cross-section of the broch

Shetland, helps our understanding of the more ruinous examples which abound elsewhere. The Broch of Mousa reaches a height of 40 feet, tapering slightly as it rises; possibly there would have been a further 6 feet of drystone masonry extending to the wall-head. In this respect Mousa is exceptional, for it has been shown that the average height of a broch was in the region of only 20 feet. There is not a single opening in the exterior wall save for the modest entrance just above ground level, so that the structure has a totally defensive appearance like a crustacean withdrawn into its shell. The space inside is remarkably constricted with almost two thirds of the diameter being occupied by the massive supporting walls. These are hollow; a device that both reduces the overall weight and provides room for a spiral staircase and galleries to ascend within the wall itself. Vertical openings in the internal wall admit a basic minimum of air and light.

Details of the internal arrangements can

Dun Telve, Glenelg – exterior of the broch

Dun Carloway, Isle of Lewis

best be studied at the more ruined brochs of Dun Carloway on Lewis and at Glenelg, where the ravages of time have conveniently laid bare cross-sections of the wall. There is no clear indication as to how a broch would have been roofed over, although the remains of a protruding ledge on the inside would point to some sort of floor or gallery. The only accommodation available as part of the broch itself consists of small cells within the wall at ground level, but some evidence of lean-to structures has been found in several brochs. Thus the internal layout strengthens the impression given by the external aspect of the broch that it was intended as a refuge in times of trouble rather than as a permanent residence.

The brochs are generally sited in the manner of farmsteads close to good arable land, and many are within easy reach of the sea. The impression that the broch builders were peaceful cultivators defending themselves against some sea-borne threat is almost inescapable. It has been suggested that the danger came from slave-traders who were constantly hunting for human supplies for the insatiable Roman market. Be that as it may, the broch must have been a perfect defence against any pirates. The Sound of Eynhallow on Orkney, with its line of brochs along both sides of the water, would have deterred all but the most determined of raiders. Surprisingly, no weapons of war have been found at any of the broch sites, but perhaps this is a further sign of the principle of passive defence.

Dun Carloway, Isle of Lewis

The unspecified dangers which gave rise to the construction of the brochs appear to have receded in the course of the third century AD, and thereafter many were converted or even demolished to make ordinary homes. Examples of this rather haphazard rebuilding can be seen at Sumburgh Head on Shetland, Gurness on Orkney, and Midhowe on Rousay. As recently as the 1870s there was still a family living in the broch of Dun Carloway on Lewis.

This remarkable, albeit short-lived, form of building shows a high degree of uniformity of design. Only two basic broch types have been identified; and according to whether the ground-galleried or the solid-based type is accepted as the ancestral broch, then the origins of the broch culture can be sought in either Skye or Orkney. The uniform style and high standard of the masonry both point to a band of professional broch-builders travelling the land in pursuit of their com-missions, rather in the manner of the master masons of the Middle Ages. Such a theory helps to explain the existence of such obvious outlying brochs as Edinshall as far south as the Borders. But for the most part the brochs occur within the area which remained beyond the reach of the Romans. Somehow the broch-builders have come to be associated with the ancestors of the Picts, adding a further dimension of mystery to that race or group of peoples who stand so dimly per-ceived at the dawn of recorded history in Scotland.

Whatever uncertainties may exist about the purpose of the brochs and the identity of their builders, all commentators agree on the uniquely Scottish nature of the phenom-enon; and some even see in the broch an early instance of that same instinct for small-scale defence which later gave rise to that other typically Scottish architectural form, the tower-house.

The Earth-house

Among the most curious remains of pre-historic Scotland are surely the subterranean stone structures known as 'earth-houses' or 'souterrains'. These have survived essentially as curved sunken passages now exposed to view, but originally they would have been roofed over and effectively concealed among the group of huts with which they were associated.

Some two hundred earth-houses have been discovered in Scotland, and from the scant evidence they have yielded, they would seem to belong to the first three centuries AD. It is generally agreed that the earth-house served primarily as an underground store, rather in the manner of a

Ardestie earth-house

cellar, but the cunning arrangement and skilful construction of these twisting passages with their hidden entrances strongly suggest that they might also have been designed as places of refuge. One can imagine them being used during a raid as a hideout by the non-fighting members of the community who would then re-emerge once the danger had passed. However, the exact function of the earth-houses remains an enigma, which is compounded by the disappearance of the huts to which they were linked, almost suggesting a race of subterranean humans.

There are excellent examples of the basic type at Ardestie, Carlungie and Tealing in Angus, where the full extent of the curved underground passages can now be viewed. On Orkney there are two slightly different specimens of the genre, Rennibister and Grain. These structures of expert drystone masonry are still roofed over. The stone lintels at Grain and stone corbelling at Rennibister have combined with pillars of stone to ensure the survival of these earth-houses over a period of almost two thousand years. Both have been built with great skill, more than the requirements of storage would warrant; but if they were actually used as refuges it is difficult to imagine that the dank and stifling darkness of these underground chambers could have been endured for long.

Carlungie earth-house

47

The Age of the Hillfort

Around the eighth century BC the first defensive works were built on strategic summits south of the Highlands. Generally known as hillforts, they remained a prominent feature of the Scottish landscape well beyond Roman times, in some cases even into the Middle Ages. The name 'fort' is something of a misnomer, since these buildings do not seem to represent military outposts in any conventional sense. Rather they were settlements protected by palisades, stone walls or earthworks. The Scottish hillforts reached their maximum number during the last centuries BC and have come to be identified as the strongholds of mainly a new wave of Celtic immigration consisting of iron-using warrior aristocracies which subjugated the indigenous population.

By about the first century AD the southeast of Scotland was bristling with hillforts. The Cheviots, on the present border with England, were the most favoured locality; here it was almost impossible to be out of sight of a hillfort. Some grew to be of considerable size. Eildon Hill North, thought to have been the capital of the Selgovae tribe, was a small city; over three hundred house sites have been found and it has been estimated that a population of two thousand people once lived here. Traprain Law, twenty miles to the east of Edinburgh, was another hillfort of note, probably the capital of the Votadini tribe. The huge whaleback hill is still an obvious landmark dominating the countryside in all directions, although a part of it has been nibbled away by quarrying operations in recent times. In 1919 a rich hoard of Roman silver was unearthed on Traprain Law. Evidently buried early in the fifth century AD, it may be assumed that the hill was still occupied at that date.

Although the evidence is not absolutely clear, it does seem that most of the hillforts were permanently occupied, and not just places of occasional refuge. There are sure signs, however, of the struggles for their possession. The phenomenon of vitrifaction may be observed at many hillforts; this

Eildon Hill North

occurred when the firing of a timber and stone structure caused the stone to fuse in the intense heat of the flames. One of the best preserved of these 'vitrified' forts is located at Finavon in Angus. But who were the aggressors in this fight for control of the hilltops? Historical circumstances point to none other than the occupants of the hillforts themselves: petty chieftains asserting their tribal authority and prestige against their neighbours. Here we can see the beginnings of the anarchic raiding, cattle-reiving and local warfare of later centuries.

Scotland's hillforts do not reward those who struggle up to their windswept summits with much in the way of archaeological remains, but the views are truly exhilarating and the tactical command of the land becomes immediately apparent. However, the hillforts were by no means impregnable bases. Even the mighty Eildon Hill North was by the end of the first century AD no longer in the hands of the natives but was occupied by the Romans who used it as a signal station – just another link in the chain of imperial communications. Altogether there are some 1,500 hillforts in Scotland, mostly in the south, which provide a mute testimony to those unsettled times when the warring Celtic tribes vied with one another and with the Romans for supremacy in the land then known to outsiders as Caledonia.

Dun Skeig, Kintyre

GAZETTEER 2

Brochs
1 Clickhimin
2 Carn Liath
3 Dun Beag
4 Dun Carloway
5 Dun Dornadilla
6 Dun Dornaigil
7 Edin's Hall
8 Glenelg
9 Gurness
10 Midhowe
11 Mousa
12 Ness of Burgi

Cairns
13 Blackhammer
14 Cairn Bann
15 Cairn Holy
16 Cairnpapple Hill
17 Cairn o'Get
18 Clava Cairns
19 Cnoc Freiceadain
20 Corriemony
21 Cuween Hill
22 Dwarfie Stane
23 Glebe
24 Grey Cairns of Camster
25 Holm of Papa Westray
26 Kilmory
27 Knowe of Yarso
28 Maes Howe
29 Memsie
30 Midhowe
31 Nether Largie
32 Quanterness
33 Quoyness
34 Ri Cruin
35 Taversoe Tuick
36 Torrylin
37 Unstan
38 Wideford Hill

Earth-houses
39 Ardestie
40 Carlungie
41 Culsh
42 Grain
43 Rennibister
44 Tealing

Hillforts
45 Barsalloch
46 Castlelaw
47 The Caterthuns
48 The Chesters
49 Dun Skeig
50 Eildon Hill North
51 Finavon
52 Mote of Mark
53 Torr a'Chaisteal
54 Traprain Law

Settlements
55 Jarlshof
56 Knap of Howar
57 Skara Brae
58 Stanydale

Stone Settings
59 Auchagallon
60 Callanish
61 Cullerlie
62 East Aquhorthies
63 Hill o'Many Stanes
64 Loanhead
65 Machrie Moor
66 Moss Farm Road
67 Ring of Brodgar
68 Stenness
69 Steinacleit
70 Temple Wood
71 Tomnaverie
72 Torhouse

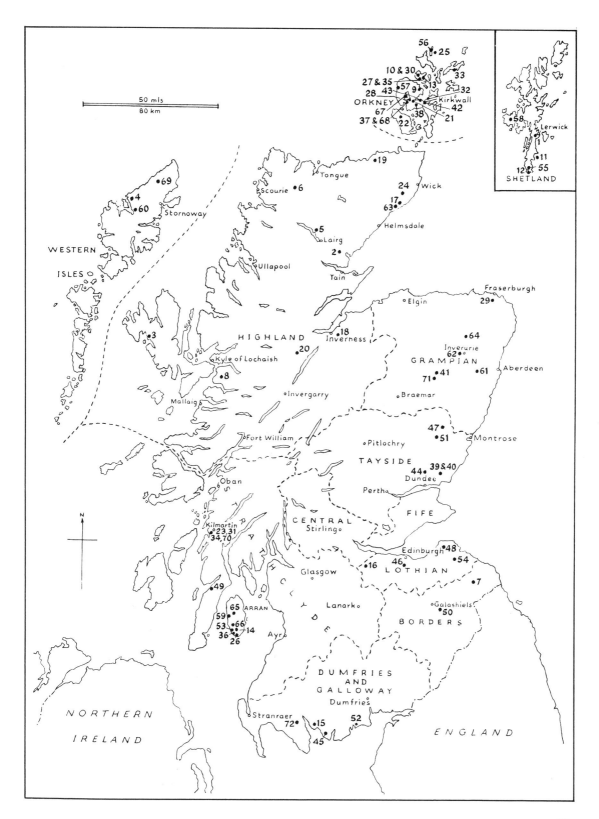

WESTERN
ISLES

●69
●4
●60
Stornoway

Tongue
Scourie ●6

HIGHLAND

Ullapool

●3

Kyle of Lochaish

●8
Mallaig

Fort William

Oban

Kilmartin
●23,31
34,70

Glasgow

●49

65
ARRAN
59
53 ●66 ●14
36 26
Ayr

Lanark

●19

Wick
24
17
63 ●
Helmsdale

●5
Lairg
2 ●
Tain

●18
Inverness
●20

Invergarry

56
●25
10 & 30
27 & 35
28 43
57 9 13
67
37 & 68
22
38
21
ORKNEY

33
32
Kirkwall
42
21

Elgin

GRAMPIAN

62
71 ●41
Braemar

47●
●51

TAYSIDE
44 ● 39&40
Dundee
Perth

CENTRAL
Stirling

FIFE

Edinburgh●48
46 ●54
16 ●
LOTHIAN
●7

Galashiels
●50
BORDERS

DUMFRIES
AND
GALLOWAY
Dumfries

Stranraer
72 ●15
45

52

ENGLAND

NORTHERN
IRELAND

Fraserburgh
29●

●64
Inverurie
●61
Aberdeen

Montrose

Pitlochry

SHETLAND
●58
Lerwick
●11
12 ●55

50 mls
80 km

N

51

3 The Triumph of the Scots

Julius Agricola's Caledonian campaign in the AD 80s brought more than the clash of Roman arms to the verge of the Highlands. It also brought Caledonia into the focus of historical scrutiny, albeit somewhat hazily at first. None other than Tacitus was the chronicler of the Roman victory at Mons Graupius in AD 84, but the actual location of the battle is still a matter of dispute. It is in the pages of Tacitus that the first named historical personality in Scotland springs to life. The defeated leader of the Caledonians, Calgacus, is credited with a speech of great dramatic potential: 'Where they make a wilderness they call it peace' are his memorable lines, which ring true in spite of their obvious invention. Whatever the degree of poetic licence which surrounds Calgacus, and whatever uncertainty exists about the precise geographical site of Mons Graupius, Scottish history in a real sense may be said to begin with them.

This does not imply that henceforth there are reliable records to guide us through the obscurity of early Scottish history. In fact the next thousand years of Scotland's development are but patchily and often ambivalently recorded. Yet the general thrust of events is clear. In the centuries following the Roman occupation four main groups of people contend for supremacy: the Picts in the north, the Angles in the south-east, the Britons of Strathclyde in the south-west and the Dalriadic Scots from Ireland, who begin their gradual advance with a modest colony in Argyll in the second half of the fifth century. In the year AD 843 it is the Scots of Dalriada who emerge victorious under their king, Kenneth MacAlpin, the first joint ruler of both Pict and Scot. But the kingdom of Scotland does not yet properly exist, for the Northern and Western Isles, together with the coastal regions of the mainland from Caithness and Sutherland to Argyll and Galloway, have fallen into the hands of the Norsemen. The first millennium of Scottish history does not bring about the making of the kingdom so much as the triumph of Dalriada over her rivals and the beginnings of Scottish unification.

To modern eyes Scotland may appear to be a homogeneous entity but at the dawn of the historical era the land was highly fragmented with several conflicting spheres of influence. It requires a different perspective to grasp the regional dimension at the time when it was the sea routes which determined the culture, outlook and development of the land regions. It has been proposed that the prehistoric structure of Scotland, which lasted well into the Middle Ages, may be broadly expressed as an Atlantic Province facing the north and west and a Continental Province facing east. Accordingly, the historical development of the Northern and Western Isles, together with their neighbouring coastal regions on the mainland, was fundamentally different from that of the central area and the east coast. Thus the basic division of Scotland was between east

Footprint on the rock at Dunadd, capital of Dalriada 53

Dumbarton Rock – ancient capital of the Britons of Strathclyde

and west rather than between north and south, with the great mountain range of Drum Alban forming an almost impenetrable barrier to communications.

The Roman invasions of the first to third centuries AD ignored the natural sea-orientated regions and aimed at a territorial conquest of Scotland. It is not surprising that the hopeless venture was so soon abandoned, for command of the sea was still the key to control of the land, as the Vikings would show 500 years later. Instead of subjugating Scotland, the Romans then opted for a policy of containment and drew an artificial line across the country at its narrowest point between the Forth and the Clyde estuaries, a 37-mile frontier which was defended by a 12-foot rampart of turves. The Antonine Wall may have looked effective on the maps of the Empire back in Rome but it cannot have meant much in terms of military strategy, for a simple boat voyage was enough to circumvent its defences. Far from providing a buffer against the barbarians of the north, it was probably no more than a minor local hindrance to those living in the vicinity. Scarcely twenty years after construction began in around AD 143 the Antonine Wall was finally abandoned in favour of Hadrian's Wall far to the south.

Nevertheless, the Romans did occupy a large part of what is modern Scotland: and south of the Highlands are many signs of their attempts to maintain a hold on the north-west frontier of the Empire. Although the nature of this partial and sporadic occupation was exclusively military, the social and commercial influence of the Romans in Scotland should not be underestimated. The introduction of a money-based economy and a rudimentary knowledge of Latin must have left some sort of impression on those who came into contact with the Romans; but probably the main legacy of the Roman period was the isolation of Scotland from the rest of Britain and the first formalised conception of a north-south division of the country.

Just as the Roman Empire was withdrawing amidst chaos and confusion from Britain in the first half of the fifth century, so Ninian, a Romanised Briton and native of Galloway, was the first Christian missionary to take the Gospel to the heathens in the north. It has been suggested that Ninian's work among the Picts was a final attempt by Rome to bring a measure of civilisation to Scotland: partly a furtherance of imperial policy under a different guise. Ninian's achievements and those of his contemporaries and immediate successors as pioneers of Christian preaching in Scotland have been obscured by the later reputation of Columba and his monastery at Iona. In archaeological terms there is little to show the work of either Ninian or Columba, but an examination of the various dedications in their respective names strongly suggests that Ninian penetrated much farther north than is generally held, perhaps even as far as Orkney and Shetland. Conversely, the scope of Columba and others from Iona appears to have been more restricted to the western seaboard and the islands of the Hebrides.

The main reason for the inflated claims of the Columban mission on Iona, which was founded around AD 563, is political rather than religious. As a prince of the blood royal of Ireland, Columba was also the champion of his compatriots, the Scots of Dalriada, who had settled in Argyll; and much of his life's energies were devoted to the promotion of their interests, notably their territorial expansion at the expense of the Picts. With the ultimate triumph of the Scots of Dalriada over the Picts in AD 843 and the unification of the two peoples under Kenneth MacAlpin it was natural that Columba's considerable deeds should be suitably amplified to match the new political circumstances. However, it should be borne in mind that the Christianisation of Scotland was altogether a more complex story than that of one man performing miracles and founding churches with super-human zeal. Kentigern, Moluag, Maelrubha and Donan, as well as Ninian, are just some of the better known names of those who braved the perils and hardships to be endured in the untamed wilderness of northern Scotland during the fifth to eighth centuries, the founding period of the Church in Scotland. It is a shame that no contemporary records have survived to document the work of these men, but their island retreats scattered throughout the Inner Hebrides and along the western seaboard are known to us through various place-names and the remains of their simple churches are presumed to lie beneath later foundations.

Under Kenneth MacAlpin the Dalriadic Scots transferred their capital from the rock at Dunadd in the west to the centre of the Pictish lands at Scone. So it was at Scone henceforth that the kings of Alba, or Scotland, took their oaths, and the footprint in the rock at Dunadd was no longer used for the purpose. Partly as a response to the depredations of the Vikings, the ecclesiastical capital was moved from Iona to Dunkeld, further underlining the finality of the Scottish takeover of the Picts. Such was the great

sanctity surrounding Iona that the burial ground on the island, known as the 'Reilig Odhrain', continued to serve as the final resting place of Scottish monarchs until the end of the eleventh century.

With the Picts, the subjects of the Scottish expansion, we encounter perhaps the greatest and most tantalising enigma in the entire history of Scotland. Although almost nothing about the Picts can be advanced with certainty, it would appear that they represented an amalgam of the prehistoric peoples of northern Scotland. Following the takeover of their territory by the Scots in the ninth century, the Picts vanished without a trace. Their language, culture and even the name by which they called themselves have been irretrievably lost, and their history as a people can only be deduced from scraps of information. Never were the Dark Ages quite so dark in terms of historical and archaeological evidence as in the case of the Picts, who constituted the basic native population of northern Scotland between the fourth and ninth centuries AD.

Were it not for their art, which was both original and accomplished, the Picts would merit no more than the occasional footnote; indeed it is largely on account of their art, in the form of mysterious symbol-stones and ornately decorated cross-slabs, that occasional glimpses may be obtained of the identity of this gifted and elusive group of people. The weird language of their symbol-stones still baffles the best minds but their naturalistic carvings convey at least some physical and material details of their lives. In these stylish reliefs the Picts appear as mounted warriors, elegant and sedate, whether riding into battle or out on a hunting expedition. Certainly, what can be deduced about their history confirms the image of a race of formidable warriors.

It is thought that the Picts came together in a loose sense as a confederacy of tribal units as a direct response to the menacing incursions of the Romans. This would have led naturally to the emergence of a common ruler, or perhaps two if there were southern and northern Picts, as maintained by the chronicler Bede, writing in the eighth century. To the Romans the Picts were known as the most ferocious of their enemies in the north. In their turn the Teutonic Angles of Northumbria also came to grief at the hands of the Picts in AD 685 at the battle of Nechtansmere. The importance of this Pictish victory, a seemingly remote clash of arms compared to other great battles of Scottish history, can hardly be overstated as a vital step towards the creation of the sovereign state of Scotland. If the Picts had not stood firm and won the day, it is more than probable that the Angles would have established themselves as the dominant power in Scotland, and much of the country would have become no more than an extension of Northumbria. The Picts should thus receive credit for the safeguarding of a national identity; for without Nechtansmere there could have been no Bannockburn. Prior to Nechtansmere the Angles were already well established in Lothian, and in fact Edinburgh was named after the Northumbrian King Edwin who had a fort constructed on the rock there in about AD 682.

The Vikings also played an indirect rôle in the formation of the Scottish kingdom. Their takeover of the Northern Isles at the end of the eighth century and their frequent and bloody harrying of the coastal regions from Sutherland and Caithness to Argyll and Galloway upset the precarious balance of power. The dominant Picts were severely weakened by the depredations of the Norsemen, while the Scots were driven further inland into Pictish territory to escape the fury of the sea-borne invaders. Perhaps the

St Martin's Cross, Iona – a fine example of early Celtic carving

Picts and Scots had a common interest in joining forces to resist the Vikings but the signs are that the emergence of Kenneth MacAlpin in AD 843 as the king of Picts and Scots did not mark a voluntary merger so much as a forced takeover of the Picts by the Scots. The resulting submergence of the Pictish identity in the ninth and tenth centuries and the great silence which surrounds the memory of the Picts to this day speaks of a cultural suppression rather than a fusion of values. One of the last testimonials of the Picts is the majestic column known as Sueno's Stone of the tenth century. The battle portrayed might have been a skirmish with the Vikings, but the possibility of hostility between Picts and Scots cannot be ruled out.

The immediate outcome of the unification of Alba under Kenneth MacAlpin was a transfer of authority from the western fringes to the geographical centre of the land. This was a significant move away from the ancient 'Atlantic Province' to a more territorial conception of Scotland, a trend that would be further emphasised under the feudal system of the Middle Ages. The birth of the nation in AD 843 also heralded the beginning of the Viking era in the Northern and Western Isles: the Norsemen consolidated their gains in these areas at the expense of the Picts and Scots respectively and retained their control for several centuries. Thus under Norse rule did the old idea of the 'Atlantic Province' survive into the late Middle Ages and Viking blood become the fifth strain to be added to that of Pict, Scot, Angle and Briton in the making of modern Scotland.

Perhaps the most lasting achievement of the new kingdom of the Scots of Dalriada was their promotion of the Irish form of Gaelic over the language of the Picts, which was perhaps the other variety of the Celtic language, which has come down to us as Welsh, combined with some pre-Celtic elements. Archaeological remains of the Dalriadic Scots are hard to identify, but perhaps the most telling symbols of the new regime are the two Irish-type round-towers at Abernethy and Brechin, once the heartland of the Picts. At Scone, the new royal centre, there is nothing to be seen as a reminder of Kenneth MacAlpin and his successors but the mound where they took their kingly oath and a disputed version of the Scottish Stone of Destiny. It would appear that the Scots' hold on the country was still disputed from within, so little effort was expended on new works.

The semi-autonomous 'mormaers' of Moray, whose most famous son was Macbeth, were the most troublesome opponents of the Scots. It is possible that Macbeth's rule from 1040 to 1057 represented a last assertion of the Pictish spirit but the power of the Scots was re-established by Malcolm Canmore of the House of MacAlpin. However, with Malcolm Canmore the supremacy of the Gael entered its final phase. Through his marriage to the English princess Margaret the door was opened for all manner of Anglo-Saxon and then Norman influences to permeate the Scottish monarchy. The unification of Scotland under native, Celtic rule finally went to rest in 1097 with the death of Donald Bane, who was the last of his dynasty to be buried in Iona, the sacred resting place of the Dalriadic kings. The triumph of the Scots of Dalriada was short-lived but it left a firm imprint, as well as its name, on the country that was coming into being.

Round tower at Abernethy. The clock is Victorian

Roman Remains

Although Roman involvement in Scotland lasted almost three hundred years from Agricola's successful campaign of AD 80, the land of Caledonia was never colonised to the same degree as the province of Britannia to the south. In effect the Roman presence in Scotland did not progress beyond a partial and fluctuating military occupation which brought with it only a limited advancement in terms of civilisation. The Roman remains in Scotland reflect the various phases of the legions' fortunes, from the initial invasion to a policy of containment, and finally withdrawal.

One of the most telling of Roman works in Scotland, in a historical sense, is the camp built at Inchtuthil some seven miles south-east of Dunkeld. Excavation has established that it was founded around AD 86 in the immediate aftermath of the Agricolan campaign which had ended with the first major defeat of the Caledonians at Mons Graupius in AD 84. The camp once covered fifty acres, and it was the only permanent legionary fortress in Scotland, capable of housing upwards of 5,000 in its orderly barracks. There remains but little to be seen today, but the interesting aspect of Inchtuthil is that due to a re-appraisal of imperial policy the camp was abandoned before it was properly completed. The discovery of nearly one million iron nails, which were buried at the site apparently in order to prevent them from falling into the hands of the enemy, speaks of a hasty withdrawal and much building still to be done.

Another of the original Agricolan camps, that at Ardoch ten miles south of Crieff, enjoyed a longer career than Inchtuthil.

Antonine Wall at Watling Lodge

Ardoch was re-used on several occasions, and there are as many as four superimposed forts on the site, extending in time from the AD 80s to the third century. Although no buildings remain, the earthworks of the fort are extremely well preserved and the rampart stands to a height of over six feet. Three gaps, which indicate the position of the gates, are clearly visible. Close by are the outlines of six overlapping marching camps which show that Ardoch retained its strategic importance on the route north right up to the final campaigns of Septimius Severus and Caracalla between AD 208 and 211. The site of Ardoch Fort today is lush farmland where cattle graze among the ramparts – a

pleasant spot to evoke memories of the legionary presence in Caledonia.

It is the Antonine Wall, however, which is the greatest monument of the Romans in Scotland. It extends for thirty-seven miles from Bo'Ness on the Forth to Old Kilpatrick on the Clyde. The Antonine Wall, constructed between AD 143 and 145, was intended as a more northerly replacement of Hadrian's Wall of about twenty years beforehand. By comparison the Antonine Wall is a modest affair, consisting of a twelve-foot turf rampart heaped up on a stone base. To the north of the wall there was a ditch, and the upcast from the digging served to form a further protective mound. A military way

Roman camp at Ardoch

ran parallel to the wall along the south side, and a score of forts provided shelter for the troops every couple of miles.

Several stretches of the Antonine Wall are still in evidence today, notably at Rough Castle and Watling Lodge between Bonnybridge and Falkirk where the profiles of the ditch and rampart are best preserved. Yet this fine work of military architecture was held by the Romans for less than twenty years in all. It was abandoned for a while from AD 158, then briefly re-occupied, only to be abandoned once more and finally in the AD 160s. What was once the wildest and remotest frontier of the Roman Empire is now the heartland of twentieth-century Scotland, a complex web of railway, canal and motorway.

Apart from the ditch and rampart, the greatest relics of the Antonine Wall are the commemorative distance slabs, of which there is a fine collection in Glasgow's Hunterian Museum. These slabs marked the completion of various stretches of the wall. Some depict the triumph of the forces of Rome over the native tribesmen, who are shown both as captives in meek submission and as soldiers cowering on the battlefield beneath the hooves of the Roman cavalry: an interesting early example of the art of political propaganda. In all, twenty of these distance slabs have been preserved, and their inscriptions provide a valuable documentary record of the construction of the Antonine Wall. Most of the slabs came to be discovered as a result of ploughing activities since the eighteenth century. It appears that they were buried in shallow pits by the departing Romans to save them from defacement by their enemies. This accounts for the relatively good state of preservation of some of the slabs which passed directly into safekeeping, but others received rough treatment and have become extremely worn in the process.

Possibly the least military of the Roman

Distance slab from the Antonine Wall (Hunterian Museum)

installations in Scotland – although it originally served a fort – is the bath-house in the
Glasgow suburb of Bearsden. The site was
excavated in 1973 in the preparation of a
housing redevelopment. Fortunately, the
foundations of the bath-house have been
preserved but the fort is now lost beneath a
complex of twentieth-century flats. Close by
the modern road follows a brief stretch of the
old military way, and its memory is recalled
in the name of Roman Road.

Knowledge of Roman Scotland is fairly
comprehensive but new discoveries are still
coming to light. Aerial photography carried
out during the dry summer of 1984 revealed
the faint outlines of four more Roman forts,
the most significant find being that of a
three-acre fort in the grounds of Drumlanrig
Castle in Dumfriesshire. It is thought unlikely, however, that any important civilian
remains of the Roman presence will be
discovered.

Distance slab from the Antonine Wall (Hunterian Museum)

St Ninian at Whithorn

Although Ninian's rôle as one of the founding fathers of the Christian Church in Scotland is often obscured by the tremendous reputation of St Columba who embarked on his mission a century later, Ninian's pioneering work was of fundamental importance, and it is to this Romano-British official, a native of Galloway, that the credit of first bringing Christianity to Scotland is due. Beneath the ruins of the twelfth-century Whithorn Priory archaeologists have identified earlier foundations which in all probability belong to Ninian's Candida Casa ('white house'). This was the very first recorded Christian missionary base in Scotland, founded in AD 397.

Tracing the actual extent of Ninian's mission is fraught with difficulties, not the least of which is the lack of contemporary documentary evidence. Writing some three centuries later, Bede ascribed to Ninian the conversion of the 'southern Picts' and to Columba that of the 'northern Picts'. But it is quite possible that Bede's grasp of Scottish geography was not accurate, for it has been shown that Ninian's mission took him much further north into the wilds of Caledonia than Columba.

Using the evidence of place-names and dedications to St Ninian which go back to the Dark Ages, it has been demonstrated that Ninian's route through Scotland followed very much in the tracks of the Roman legions who had attempted in vain to tame the Highlands. Ninian's trail, beginning at Whithorn in the south-west, continued via Glasgow, Stirling and Strathmore to the rocky promontory of Dunnottar overlooking the North Sea just south of Stonehaven. Thence, via Aberdeenshire to the Great Glen, Ninian headed further north, leaving

St Ninian's Cave near Physgill

a memory of his passing at Glen Urquhart by Loch Ness in Cill an Trinnian (St Ninian's Cell). There is evidence of Ninian's missionary activity on the Scottish mainland as far north as Navidale on the east coast of Sutherland. It is tempting to extend Ninian's travels to Shetland where there is a beautiful St Ninian's Isle with remains of a pre-Norse church, but conclusive proof is lacking.

Not far from Ninian's Candida Casa at Whithorn there are two other sites which have a personal association with the saint. There is the tiny chapel at Isle of Whithorn, and a few miles along the coast at Physgill is St Ninian's Cave which served as a retreat for solitude and meditation. These sites are as sacred as any of greater renown elsewhere in Scotland.

Following Ninian's death in AD 432 the work at Whithorn was maintained, and there are several indications in the vicinity to suggest a measure of lingering cultural influence of the departed Romans. At Kirkmadrine, in the Rhins of Galloway, there are three of the oldest Christian memorial stones in Britain dating back to the fifth or early sixth century. They bear inscriptions in the Greek characters of the time, exhibiting the 'Chi-Rho' symbol, which stands for the first two letters of Christ's name, and the Latin 'hic iacit', or 'here lies' formula, commonly found on Christian tombs throughout Europe. It would thus appear that Scotland's very first encounter with Christianity, through Ninian's mission at Whithorn, occurred in the context of Rome's declining power. It has been suggested that Ninian's preaching of the Gospels might well have been part of an overall policy by Flavius Stilicho, who was ruler of the Western Empire from AD 395 to 408, to win through the promotion of the Christian faith what the Romans had failed to conquer by the sword.

The Ruthwell Cross

The seventh-century Ruthwell Cross, which stands some eighteen foot high in an apse of Ruthwell Church in Dumfriesshire, is a unique example on Scottish soil of a style of sculptural excellence quite different to the great crosses of Celtic and Pictish inspiration. The anonymous sculptor has created one of the most accomplished Early Christian monuments in Europe, drawing on elements of Hellenistic artistic tradition, a fact which proclaims that Scotland in the Dark Ages was not without its bursts of dazzling light. There is a tendency to think of the first centuries of Christianity in Scotland, prior to the majestic works of Anglo-Norman style, as lacking in sophistication, but the Ruthwell Cross, with its rich and confident sculptural scenes, gives the lie to any such notion of archaic simplicity. Its four faces are abundant in the finest carvings which appear almost to leap out of the stone shaft of the cross commanding the onlooker's attention.

The north face portrays John the Baptist, Christ glorified, Christ breaking bread in the desert, and the flight into Egypt. On the south face are the Crucifixion, the Annunciation, Christ healing the blind man, Mary Magdalene washing Christ's feet, and the Visitation. On the east and west faces there are carvings of rampant foliage with birds and animals. Around the outer edge of the panels runs a remarkable poem in Anglian runes, a highly moving narration of the Crucifixion.

The naturalistic figurative art of the Ruthwell Cross, like that of the Pictish cross-slabs, was not totally absorbed into the mainstream of Scottish religious sculpture, which was to find its noblest expression in the great high crosses of predominantly abstract design in the Middle Ages. The spirit of figurative sculpture lived on, however, making its reappearance several centuries later in such disparate works as Rosslyn Chapel and the grave slabs of the West Highland chiefs.

The Ruthwell Cross – Mary Magdalene (below) *and Christ Glorified* (right)

Columba's Mission on Iona

Columba is reported to have arrived in Iona from his native Ireland in the year AD 563 when he was already forty-two. As a great-great-grandson of the famous High King of Ireland, Niall of the Nine Hostages, Columba was no ordinary Christian missionary. Nor was his journey entirely motivated by Christian idealism: he was in fact sailing into political exile as a result of his rôle in what amounted to a minor civil war. His later achievements in the cause of Christianity should be viewed in the light of his royal origins and his commitment; it was these factors which led him to strive consistently on behalf of his kinsmen, that group of Dalriadic Scots which had implanted them-selves in the western part of the country today known as Argyll.

Although tradition has it that Columba proceeded directly from Ulster to Iona, there are signs that he stopped *en route* close to the Mull of Kintyre, where footsteps in a rock near the beach are said to mark the spot where he first landed on Scottish soil. There is also the place known as St Columba's Cave on the west shore of Loch Killisport which contains carved crosses and a rock altar. According to local belief Columba stayed in this cave for some time in order to consider his next move. Be that as it may, it was to Iona that Columba eventually came and where he founded his monastery.

Again there is an element of doubt as to whether Columba's was the first Christian mission on Iona, for there are historical references to a college of seven bishops already on the island, and it is recorded that on his landing Columba was met by two of

St Columba's Cave near Ellary

them who attempted to persuade him to go elsewhere. Evidently, Columba stood his ground.

Those in search of Columba's presence on Iona will find that nothing is visible of his original monastery but the vallum or rampart which once marked its overall extent. A modest monastic settlement in the early Irish fashion can be imagined, with the little community housed in simple huts of wood or wattle. There may also have been some cells of drystone with beehive vaulting, like those which can still be seen on Eileach an Naoimh, one of the tiny group of islands

known as the Garvellachs in the Firth of Lorn. There are various Columban associations with Eileach an Naoimh; the monastery is said to have been founded by Columba's uncle and the island is also claimed as the burial place of Eithne, Columba's mother.

On Iona itself there are, naturally enough, several places which are associated with memories of Columba's life. Torr an Aba, an outcrop of rock facing the west front of the thirteenth-century Benedictine Abbey, is reputed to have been the location of the saint's cell where he would have slept, using a stone for his pillow. Columba's Bay or Port na Curaich – 'harbour of the skin-covered boat' – on the west of the island is the traditional landing-place of Columba, and there is a more uncertain identification of Cobhan Cuilteach – 'the remote hollow' – as the spot where Columba used to withdraw for prayer. At the Abbey proper there is St Columba's Shrine, to the north of the west doorway, reputed to be the site of the saint's tomb which was later removed to Dunkeld away from the threat of the Viking marauders.

As for Columba's mission, there are records of two journeys to the Pictish King Brude MacMaelchon at Inverness but, given the hostility between the Picts and the Dalriadic Scots, these might well have been diplomatic as well as religious missions. The exact extent of Columba's missionary activity is difficult to determine; and there is a strong argument that it was in the main restricted to the areas in the west in or adjacent to the colony of Dalriada, with its capital on the rock near Crinan known as Dunadd. The later and lasting glory of Iona is doubtless linked to the ultimate triumph of the Scots over the Picts, which greatly enhanced the prestige and achievements of Columba, to the virtual exclusion of the other founding fathers of the Christian Church in Scotland such as Ninian, Kentigern, Moluag and Maelrubha – to name but a few.

Nevertheless, Iona's renown and influence as a holy place are almost entirely to the credit of Columba; that Iona today is more of a national shrine than St Andrews must ultimately be ascribed to his work and example. This is entirely as Columba himself had foreseen it, according to the last message

The restored cloister of Iona Abbey

addressed to his fellow monks as recorded by Adamnan, his seventh-century biographer, the ninth Abbott of Iona: 'Small and mean though this place is, yet it shall be held in great and unusual honour, not only by Scotic Kings and people, but also by rulers of foreign and barbarous nations and by their subjects; the Saints even of other Churches shall regard it with no common reverence.'

Columba's reference to 'the rulers of foreign and barbarous nations' was probably aimed at the much maligned Picts and clearly shows that the great saint remained also a politician to the last. However, it is the more charitable and Christian aspects of his life and works which have kept alive his memory and his spirit. Iona today is not just a museum-cum-shrine but a vital centre of continuing evangelical activity.

Iona Abbey with the Reilig Odhrain in the foreground

The Sites of Early Christianity

In the popular imagination Iona is the foremost of the early Christian sites in Scotland; but in the first centuries of the new faith there were several other independent missions in the country, just as there were saints other than Columba who took the Gospel to the people. These founding fathers of Christianity were – almost without exception – drawn to the seemingly remote islands strung along the western seaboard. Remoteness is, however, a judgement based on our present motorised and urban perception of the land; travel in Scotland in the first century was much easier by boat, and indeed remained so for centuries. These tiny islands in the west offered to the early saints the double advantage of convenient retreats with speedy sea communications to the scattered settlements of the coast and sea lochs.

Most of the early Christian foundations of the fourth to ninth centuries have disappeared without trace, except for the name of the dedication, often buried beneath later structures. On the island of Lismore, at the entrance to Loch Linnhe to the north of Oban, was the sixth-century mission of St Moluag, the great rival of St Columba. Moluag's foundation is now obscured by the fourteenth-century church which still bears the name of the saint. In fact the church was once a cathedral, the seat of the archbishopric of Argyll; clearly the island was not considered too remote a location to have been honoured in this way.

St Donan has given his name to a number of foundations; it was at Kildonnan on the island of Eigg that Donan and the entire monastic community were reported to have been massacred in about the year AD 618. A small island in Loch Maree was the retreat of St Maelrubha in the sixth century. At Kildalton on Islay, the presence of a magnifi-

Eynhallow, Orkney

cent eighth-century cross is proof of an early Christian settlement of no mean artistic accomplishment. Oronsay would appear to have been named after the same Oran who is commemorated in the chapel and burial ground on Iona, although there is no trace of an earlier foundation than the beautiful fourteenth-century Augustinian priory. Likewise the Orkney island of Eynhallow ('sacred isle') seems an obvious candidate for a Christian mission, perhaps going back to the time of St Ninian, but the existing ruins are of a remarkably intact twelfth-century Cistercian monastery. But other indications of early Christianity on Orkney are to be found at Brough of Deerness and Brough of Birsay, both typical sites, being a rocky promontory and a tidal island respectively.

The preference for islands or promontories also applies to Ninian's Isle of Whithorn settlement. However, this closeness to the sea left the early Christian monasteries exposed and defenceless in the face of the savage attacks of the Vikings which began at the end of the eighth century. Iona, the jewel in the crown, was looted at least six times between AD 795 and 986; and it was as a result of these depredations that Columba's remains were moved, along with the seat of ecclesiastical authority, to the relative safety of Dunkeld.

It is tempting to imagine almost every windswept skerry and damp cave in the Inner Hebrides as being the sanctuary of one or other of the early saints of Scotland. Indeed, the whole idea of the first Christian churches in Scotland is tightly bound up with images of the blue skies, rocky shores and sandy coves of the Western Isles; and the distant views over the sea to the mountains of the Pictish realms must have presented a seemingly impassable barrier.

Isle of Eigg, Inner Hebrides

The Art of the Picts

A great mystery surrounds the existence and identity of the Picts. Their name is entirely due to a Roman reference to Picti in AD 297, which is usually taken to mean quite literally 'the painted ones', because of their supposed habit of tattooing their bodies. However, there is now a measure of doubt about even this simple derivation, and even if it is correct the fact remains that we do not know what the Picts called themselves. It can be stated with some confidence that the Picts represent a mixture of several racial strains, a blend of Celtic and non-Celtic elements in the population which inhabited nearly all of Scotland north of the Forth-Clyde line at about the time of the Roman invasion. In a strict historical sense they only come into being in around AD 300, following the Roman reference to the Picti, and vanish from view in the middle of the ninth century with the takeover of their kingdom by the Dalriadic Scots from Ireland, who had been gradually colonising Scotland since the fifth century.

There is an obvious need for caution about Roman references to the Picts since they are generally dismissed as 'barbarians' – the usual way of denigrating all those groups who opposed the passage of Rome. Unfortunately, no native Pictish literature is known to balance the bias of the propaganda; and were it not for the survival of numerous examples of their highly accomplished and individualistic art, it is quite likely that the Picts would have disappeared from the record almost without trace, exciting the curiosity of none but the most obscurely minded academics.

As it is, however, the quality and power of Pictish art is such that we are compelled to take seriously the existence of the Picts as a national identity of great significance. A vital and original form of sculpture, of which some 250 examples are known, is the main medium in which the art of the Picts has come down to us, and it is a testimony at once both familiar and bizarre. Although the Christian cross and allied iconography appear as the dominant feature of the great flourishing of Pictish sculpture during the eighth century there is also so much of a symbolism seemingly non-biblical in inspiration that the spectator stands confronted with a world of images more ancient and mysterious – a last glimpse of pagan forces perhaps.

The Pictish cross-slab in the churchyard at Aberlemno is a stunning example of this cultural ambivalence. One side of the slab is dominated by the cross with an ornate design of circles and geometric shapes but the vacant space has been filled with an amazing mythological menagerie including horses with fishtails, serpents with horse legs and a strange animal – a recurrent feature of Pictish symbolism – known as the 'swimming elephant' or 'Pictish beast'. The other side of the slab is a masterpiece of a naturalistic portrayal of a battle, involving both mounted warriors and foot soldiers. Both the high quality of the relief carving and the overall artistic concept are somehow reminiscent of the art of the Assyrians. The true connection is likely, however, to lie closer to home, for it is thought that a tapestry design, not dissimilar from that later employed on the Bayeux Tapestry, may have provided the model for the Aberlemno battle scene.

The Aberlemno stone also bears one of the favourite abstract Pictish symbols, known as the Z-rod and disc. Others are the V-rod and crescent, the mirror and comb, as well as a number of combinations. Together with the curious collection of beasts they form the stock imagery of Pictish sculpture.

To our eyes these symbols appear to bear no relationship to the Christian cross, and it appears on many Pictish slabs that the cross itself is perhaps almost a pretext for the symbols. It is a well known phenomenon that pagan features are often blended with Christian imagery to provide a form of cultural bridge, and it is thus safe to assume that there was no conflict in meaning – at

Pictish sculptured stone at Aberlemno

least for the Picts – between their ancient symbols and the cross.

The oldest Pictish symbol-stones, which date back to the seventh century, occur on undressed slabs without the cross and might have served as a type of territorial marker.

Only a relatively small number of burials have been discovered in association with the symbol-stones, so their possible function as grave-markers has been discounted.

Examples of the symbol-stones and cross-slabs have helped to define the probable extent of the Pictish domains. A wide distribution of a standard stock of symbols and imagery from as far south as Fife to the Western and Northern Isles is a sign of a considerable degree of cultural and political cohesion of the Picts.

Many of the Pictish stones may be seen in their original positions, or at least where they were discovered, and there are also two important collections in areas where a large number have turned up. One is at St Vigean's close to Arbroath; and the other at Meigle in Perthshire contains probably the

richest array of carvings, from biblical sources, such as the story of Daniel in the Lion's Den, to exotic beasts, such as one that can only be described as a camel, and some fine naturalistic portrayals of a mounted hunting party similar in style to the Aberlemno battle-scene.

The most singular Pictish carving of them all is Sueno's Stone just outside Forres. This mighty column, twenty feet high, is decorated with a cross on one side but the other displays a remarkable sculptural gallery. The clash of serried ranks of warriors and the

Pictish sculptured stone at Glamis

piles of the dead by what appears to be a broch celebrate a military encounter of at least one thousand years ago. The absence of the familiar Pictish symbols is perhaps a sign that the Pictish identity had already been largely absorbed by the Scots. It is one of the most frustrating aspects of Scottish archaeology and history that the mystery surrounding this and all other works of the Picts is unlikely ever to be dispelled.

Sueno's Stone at Forres

GAZETTEER 3

Ancient Kingdoms and Settlements
1 Doonhill Homestead
2 Dumbarton Rock
3 Dunadd
4 Scone

Sites and Relics of Early Christianity
5 Brough of Birsay
6 Brough of Deerness
7 Burghead Well
8 Eileach an Naoimh
9 Eynhallow
10 Inchkenneth
11 Iona
12 Kildalton Cross, Islay
13 Kildonnan, Eigg
14 Kirkmadrine Stones
15 Loch Maree
16 Laggangairn Stones
17 Lismore
18 Ruthwell Cross
19 St Columba's Cave
20 St Columba's Footsteps
21 St Fillan's Cave
22 St Ninian's Cave
23 St Ninian's Isle, Shetland
24 Whithorn Priory (Candida Casa)

Early Churches
25 Abernethy Round Tower
26 Brechin Round Tower
27 Chapel Finian

Pictish Sculptured Stones
28 Aberlemno
29 Brandsbutt
30 Dunfallandy
31 Dyce
32 Eassie
33 Fowlis Wester
34 Glamis
35 Knocknagael
36 Maiden Stone
37 Meigle
38 Picardy Stone
39 St Orland's Stone
40 St Vigean's
41 Sueno's Stone

Roman Remains
42 Antonine Wall at Castlecary
43 Antonine Wall at Rough Castle
44 Antonine Wall at Seabegs Wood
45 Antonine Wall at Watling Lodge
46 Ardoch Camp
47 Ardunie Signal Station
48 Bearsden Bathhouse
49 Burnswark
50 Distance slabs in Hunterian Museum
51 Inchtuthil Camp
52 Kinneil Fortlet
53 Muir o'Fauld Signal Station

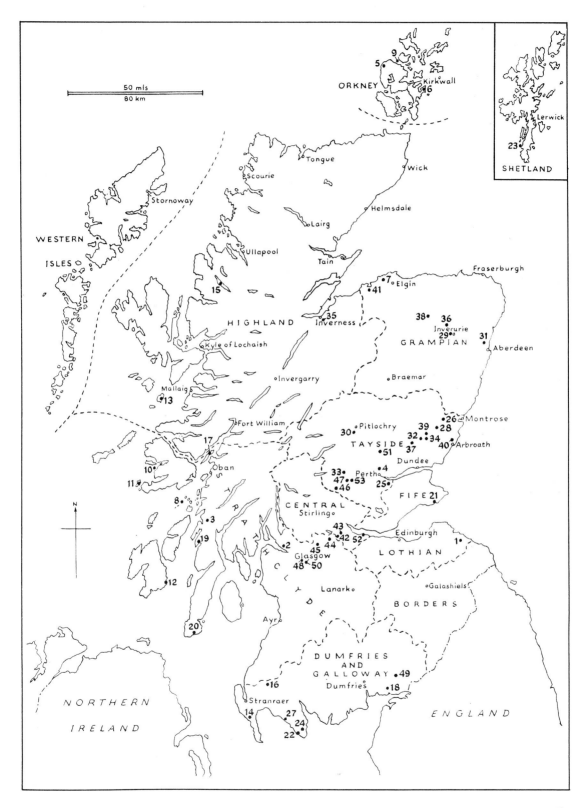

50 mls
80 km

SHETLAND

ORKNEY

WESTERN
ISLES

HIGHLAND

GRAMPIAN

TAYSIDE

CENTRAL

FIFE

LOTHIAN

BORDERS

DUMFRIES
AND
GALLOWAY

NORTHERN
IRELAND

ENGLAND

79

dwellings which are still occupied. Perhaps the most thoroughly vandalised is Scone Abbey, which is no longer even listed as an ancient monument, since it is now no more than scattered masonry in the grounds of Scone Palace. This was a direct result of the mob fury aroused by John Knox's tirade against idolatry delivered in the nearby St John's Kirk in Perth in 1559.

Despite the overall picture of monastic ruin their is one sign of life, a lonely heart beating in a mass of broken masonry. In 1948 a small Benedictine community re-occupied the ruins of Pluscarden Priory, so that the spirit of mediaeval monasticism hangs on in Scotland by a thread.

William Wallace and Robert the Bruce – In Memoriam

It is a curious fact that neither of Scotland's two great freedom-fighters and national heroes came from the heartland of the country, the realms of Dalriada and Pictland united by Kenneth MacAlpin in the ninth century. Wallace, as his name indicates, was a descendant of the Britons of Strathclyde, Bruce was a descendant of a Norman knight Sir Robert de Brus who received his lands in Annandale in 1141 from David I. This is significant in that it shows how by the thirteenth century the various ethnic strains had come to feel a strong sense of nationhood. Patriotic fervour lay dormant, however, until Scotland's sovereignty was attacked by Edward 1, the 'Hammer of the Scots'; and it was such exceptional circumstances which launched both Wallace and Bruce on their struggle for national independence.

The career of William Wallace was but a prelude to that of Robert the Bruce. Despite his famous victory in 1297 at Stirling Bridge the life and work of Wallace ended on a note of failure and anguish; in 1305 he was hung, drawn and quartered at Smithfield in London, convicted for treason to a king (Edward I) to whom he had never sworn allegiance. The ignominious end of Wallace perhaps encouraged the monument-makers of later generations to make amends. Scotland's most imposing memorial is dedicated to his memory. The Wallace Monument near Stirling is the epitome of its kind; a 220-foot stone structure perched atop a rocky eminence some 300 feet above the surrounding plain points to the heavens. The structure is like a slender, elongated tower-house, with a crown spire with a huge bronze statue of Wallace holding sword aloft set on a corner ledge. The suggestion seems

to be that Wallace is about to be launched into some Victorian Valhalla. This great work, completed in 1870, was part of the nineteenth-century revival of interest in William Wallace; the 113-foot Wallace Tower in Ayr was constructed in 1828; and several heroic statues of Wallace were set up in the Victorian period, of which a fine example was unveiled in Aberdeen in 1888. The birthplace of Wallace, thought to be at Elderslie near Paisley, is marked by a modern memorial.

It is a strange phenomenon by contrast that the supposed birthplace of Robert the Bruce at Turnberry Castle on the Ayrshire coast is not even graced with a plaque. The scant ruins of the castle lie in complete anonymity next to the famous golf course and the lighthouse. It is also curious that the memory of Bruce cannot be related to any castle he built; rather the opposite is the case, for it was his policy when he recaptured any Scottish castle from the English to demolish its fortifications and thus render it useless for re-occupation by his enemies. But the scene of Bruce's greatest triumph is his true memorial. The site of the Battle of Bannockburn (1314), just south of Stirling, has been preserved as a national shrine, although part of the historic site has been lost to modern development. It was as recently as 1964 that the striking equestrian statue of Bruce was unveiled. Another fine statue was set up at the entrance to Edinburgh Castle in 1929.

In the south-west of Scotland, in what is now Galloway Forest Park, are two huge boulders which mark notable encounters won by Bruce during a spell of guerrilla-style fighting prior to Bannockburn. Since the natural woodland of oak and birch has now almost totally been replaced by impenetrable stands of conifers it is difficult to imagine how Bruce and his desperate band of men were able to move about the country, striking at the enemy and melting back into the cover of the forest.

Unlike Wallace, the guerrilla-leader Bruce lived to be King of Scotland and

Wallace Monument near Stirling

Statue of Robert the Bruce, Bannockburn

turned out to be a progressive constitutional monarch, holding frequent parliaments. Cambuskenneth Abbey near Stirling, of which a tower still stands, was the scene of the famous parliament of 1326, the first to include both Scottish nobility and burgh representatives.

As for Bruce's grave, there is a brass plaque of 1818 marking the place of his interment in Dunfermline Abbey. At his own request his heart had been removed from his body and was to be taken by Sir James Douglas to Jerusalem on a posthumous crusade. However, Sir James was killed in a skirmish in Spain on the journey out; and legend has it that Bruce's heart was then brought back to Scotland and buried at Melrose Abbey. The truth of the matter cannot be proven for the location of the burial has escaped detection.

Cubbie Roo's Castle, Wyre, Orkney

Norse Heritage

While Anglo-Norman feudalism had been infiltrating Scotland steadily from the south, vast areas on the periphery of the country remained beyond the reach of the new social order and were subsequently unaffected by the turmoil of the Wars of Independence.

The Northern and Western Isles as well as large tracts of the corresponding coastal regions had fallen under the control of the Norsemen. Since their initial bloody raids in the ninth century the Vikings had returned in the guise of settlers and led an existence which was a curious mixture of legitimate trade and conventional farming along with their habitual piracy and raiding.

The influence of the Vikings was especially strong in the 'Nordreys' (Orkney and Shetland) and also in the 'Sudreys' (Hebrides), and a glance at the place-names on the map confirms this. From the peaks on the Isle of Rhum known as Hallival and Askivall to Muckle Flugga in the far north of Shetland there is an abundance of names deriving from the Norse language. Even on the mainland there is ample evidence of place-names which illustrate the Norse dominion. How else could Scotland's second most northerly county be called Sutherland? It is a further measure of the Norse influence that the great warrior who led the Gaelic revival in the twelfth century, thereby ensuring the Celtic supremacy of the Lords of the Isles, bore the Viking name Somerled, meaning 'summer rover'. However, the Norse language soon gave way in the Hebrides to Gaelic; but it lingered on in Orkney and Shetland until the nineteenth century, and it has bequeathed a rich vocabulary to the local dialects of those islands.

Norse control over the Western Isles lasted until 1266, and over the Northern Isles until 1472, so that they remained outposts of Norse culture for the greater part of the mediaeval period. Yet despite the centuries of Norse dominion there is surprisingly little of a specific Norse character in terms of architecture and archaeology to remind us of their presence. The magnificent cathedral of St Magnus at Kirkwall, founded in 1137 by Jarl Rognvald, lay under the jurisdiction of Trondheim in Norway, but its architecture was in the international, Anglo-Norman style of the day. Likewise the Orkney churches at Orphir and on Egilsay were imitations of foreign styles. There is in fact at first glance an amazing absence of a Norse architectural heritage where we should most expect it, namely on Orkney, which became the centre of the Atlantic traffic and a vital springboard *en route* to Ireland during its heyday in the twelfth century under the Norse earls such as Thorfinn the Mighty.

The nearest we come to a standing structure of Norse character is on the tiny Orkney island of Wyre, where a church and a castle stand in close proximity. The church, a twelfth-century work of uncertain dedication, was presumably built by the same Norse family whose castle is adjacent. This bears the strange name of Cubbie Roo's Castle, a local corruption of Kolbein Hruga, an eminent Norwegian of the mid-twelfth century whose stronghold on Wyre is mentioned in the *Orkneyinga Saga*. This structure is considered by some to be the oldest stone castle in Scotland.

Some isolated examples of Viking burials have also been found on Orkney, at Pierowall on Westray, and at Westness on Rousay. At the Bay of Kiloran, on the Hebridean island of Colonsay, a lavish ninth-century Viking warrior interment was discovered complete with horse, weapons and ornaments of the man laid to rest in his boat.

Probably the most significant of the Norse remains in Scotland are the modest foundations of typical family homes which have been excavated at Jarlshof on Shetland and on the Brough of Birsay which was the headquarters of the Orkney earldom prior to its transfer to Kirkwall. These ruins represent a new form of rectangular housing, comprising in essence a single long dwelling. This came to supplant the oval and circular houses of the Celtic peoples, and took over as the standard type of Scottish rural home from the black-house of the Hebrides to the cottages of the Lowlands. Thus the long, low houses, still so typical of the Scottish countryside today, may be traced back directly to the Norse houses first introduced to Scotland over one thousand years ago. It is not without irony that the most lasting aspect of the Norse heritage in Scotland should be something so domestic as the shape of a simple home, for the Norsemen are more famous on account of their raiding and the superb seafaring quality of their longships, which have left their mark on the design of traditional Shetland boats.

Skipness Castle, Kintyre

Castles of Stone

The timber constructions on mounds of earth, known as the 'motte and bailey', which had been introduced by the Anglo-Normans, did not evolve further as such, but in the course of the thirteenth century gave way to more durable structures of stone. The idea of the Norman keep, such as can be seen in England in Rochester and London, did not make an appearance in Scotland; a fact that probably underlines the peaceful nature of the Anglo-Norman takeover.

Some of the mottes were later fortified with stone walls as at the Peel Ring of Lumphanan and the Doune of Invernochty; and at Duffus a stone tower or keep was erected in the fourteenth century but with unfortunate results, for the earthwork was not able to bear the load and a corner of the tower collapsed in a landslide. Thus the sites of motte and bailey proved unsuitable to carry the enormous burden of masonry, and firmer foundations had to be sought for the new generation of castles. Yet the basic notion of the motte and bailey did not altogether expire, in that the timber tower and palisade can be seen as the prototype of the castle of enclosure with its keep and curtain wall of stone.

There is still a degree of uncertainty about the exact time and manner of the change in technology from timber to stone. Castle Sween in Kintyre, which possesses

Kildrummy Castle

architectural characteristics of the late eleventh century, is generally accepted as the oldest stone castle at least on the mainland. It would appear to be in the tradition of the keep style of castle rather than the courtyard type. Although Castle Sween is remarkably free of the later additions which so often obscure the original identity of many a castle, its majestic setting by the sea is considerably marred by a caravan park camped round it like a besieging army. Rothesay Castle on the Isle of Bute is a unique example of an early mediaeval circular courtyard castle where the curtain wall of stone appears to imitate the older form of the palisade. Rothesay Castle also provides the earliest authenticated case of a siege in Scotland, being that related for the year 1230 in Hakon Hakonsson's saga as a successful Norse operation.

However, the main achievement of castellar construction in Scotland in the thirteenth century can best be witnessed at three great castles, less marginal than Sween and Rothesay; Kildrummy in Aberdeenshire, Bothwell in Lanarkshire, and Dirleton in East Lothian together represent the most accomplished works of military architecture in Scotland before the Wars of Independence came to plunge the land into turmoil.

Bothwell Castle

Doune Castle

Kildrummy Castle was constructed during the reign of Alexander II (1214-49) and that of Alexander III (1249-86) with a strategic eye to the recently pacified province of Moravia (Moray), a stronghold of Celtic feeling. This new work was begun more than a mile from the site of the previous 'motte' of Kildrummy, which had been purely of local importance. The original design of the new stone castle conformed to the highest standards of the day; its lofty curtain wall with flanking towers of massive masonry enclosed spacious domestic apartments as well as an elegant chapel. The present state of the ruins bears witness to the rôle it played during the Wars of Independence, for Kildrummy Castle was besieged in 1306 by the future Edward II. During the English occupation an imposing and elaborate gatehouse, similar to the Edwardian castles of North Wales, was added to the existing fortification. Kildrummy suffered further depredations during the civil wars of the seventeenth century and was largely dismantled following the Jacobite rising of 1715. Nevertheless, the ruins do convey a powerful idea of the original thirteenth-century castle; and the beauty of the natural site on a bend of the upper reaches of the River Don has come down intact through the ages.

An even more majestic natural setting is occupied by Bothwell Castle, perched on a hill overlooking the Clyde and surrounded by fields and woodland which belie its proximity to Glasgow of only seven miles. A measure of Bothwell's stylistic merit can be gained from the usually restrained prose of the official HMSO guidebook: '. . . the grandest piece of secular architecture that the Middle Ages have bequeathed to us in Scotland. Boldly conceived, masterfully designed, and superbly executed in the finest polished ashlar masonry it ranks fully equal to the best contemporary work in England and France.' However, the signs are that the full design was never completed and that Bothwell Castle fell victim to the destructive forces unleashed by the Wars of Independence.

In spite of the excellence of its construction the castle fell in 1301 to Edward I after a siege of less than one month. It was

re-occupied by the Scots after victory at Bannockburn in 1314, and in accordance with the policy of Robert the Bruce the fortifications would have been dismantled. In 1336–7 there was a further re-occupation by the English and some restoration, but Bothwell was again dismantled by the Scots. A second restoration occurred soon after 1362 when the castle entered the possession of Archibald the Grim, 3rd Earl of Douglas. The great donjon or keep, together with the south-east portion of the curtain wall, survive to demonstrate the original quality and scale of the masonry.

Dirleton Castle's evolution is a similar tale; taken by Edward I's forces in 1298, it was occupied by the English until 1311. When it once more fell into Scottish hands it also suffered substantial demolition of its fortifications. Of the thirteenth-century work only the south-west group of towers has survived and the present gatehouse is a fourteenth-century addition by the Halyburton family, who succeeded the De Vaux as the masters of Dirleton. Further additions were made by the Ruthvens in the sixteenth century.

In terms of castellar typology Dirleton, Bothwell and Kildrummy illustrate the early development of the curtain-wall defences with the stress on both the keep and the gatehouse as the strongpoints of the castle. Caerlaverock Castle in Dumfriesshire shows a combination of the two in its massive keep-gatehouse of 1290, the first of its kind in Scotland. This merging of the keep and gatehouse is most dramatically evident at Doune Castle and at Tantallon which represent the final flourish of the curtain-wall style of castle of enclosure in the fourteenth century.

Doune Castle in Perthshire is remarkable as the most perfectly preserved specimen of fourteenth-century architecture in Scotland and it conveys more than any other the feeling of everyday life at the time. The lord's bedroom, dining-hall and living-room, the retainers' hall, guest rooms and

kitchen are surprisingly intact, as is the enclosing wall which surrounds the court-yard. Tantallon Castle in East Lothian is more ruinous but a more powerful location for a castle could hardly be imagined. Set on a steep promontory with its back to the sea, Tantallon has only to defend itself against frontal assaults. Its massive wall with a keep-gatehouse at the centre is further protected by a series of ditches and out-works of formidable strength. The solid bulk of the keep-gatehouse has been interpreted as a device of the Douglas barons for pro-tecting themselves against any treachery from within, for it became increasingly common in the fourteenth century for large castles to be manned by military retainers

Tioram Castle

or mercenaries, whose loyalties could be bought and sold.

Owing to different circumstances on the western seaboard a group of thirteenth-century castles, of which the foremost are Dunstaffnage, Mingarry and Tioram, have survived in a less ruinous state than those in the east. It appears that Bruce's policy of dismantling fortifications did not apply in the west where he needed the castles as bastions against his implacable enemies, the House of Lorn and their kinsmen the Comyns. These castles represent the consolidation of the hold of the Scottish monarchy following the cession of the Isles by Norway in 1266. The grandeur of Castle Tioram's setting on a rocky tidal island in

Loch Moidart is particularly eloquent. Other castles in the west which go back to this period are Kisimul perched on a rock in the main port of the Outer Hebridean island of Barra, which has recently been restored by the Clan Chief of the MacNeills of Barra; and Dunvegan on Skye and Duart on Mull, both of which contain vestiges of the original thirteenth-century structures disguised behind much later work. These romantically located castles all played a prominent role in the semi-autonomous Lordship of the Isles which held out for a time as the last stronghold of the Gaelic speaking Celtic culture of the old kingdom of Dalriada against the steady advance of the central monarchy.

109

The Tower-house

Whereas in England the need for castles was to die out by the end of the fourteenth century, in Scotland the continuing turmoil or 'sturt and strife' ensured that fortified residences remained commonplace until the end of the sixteenth century. But the great courtyard castles with their curtaian walls had had their day; and the new generation of 'houses of fence' introduced the concept of vertical living as a more economical means of safeguarding their occupants. The Scottish tower-house evolved as a natural response to a variety of factors, not the least of which was the royal discouragement of castle building which might serve the future purpose of the enemy to the south. The tower-houses were thus more modest structures than the great mediaeval castles and demonstrate an almost total self-reliance in design, so that

Cawdor Castle

they usher in the beginning of a truly
national form of architecture.

In its simplest manifestation the tower-
house was simply a vertical rendering of the
hall-house. A stone barrel-vaulted base-
ment supported a high vaulted room, which
served as the hall, and above that was the
solar or lord's chamber. In order to
carry the great weight of the masonry the
walls had to be very thick, and it was
common for them to measure eight feet or
more. Within the thickness of the walls a
wheel stair gave access to the various
levels, and later on extra accommodation

was gained by hewing out tiny chambers in
the solid stone.

There are not many obvious examples of
the earliest fourteenth-century versions of
the tower-house, for these structures were
often incorporated into later buildings,
thereby disguising them. Thus Crichton,
Craigmillar and even Glamis all conceal an
original tower-house. At Cawdor Castle the
tower-house, now with elegant windows,
can be more easily discerned, flanked by
later wings. But the most evident survival
of a tower-house alongside more recent
buildings is at Drum Castle. Although

Drum Castle

attached to a seventeenth-century mansion and pierced by a large mock-Gothic window, the tower at Drum has retained its original martial appearance. Its primitive style of battlements with high merlons is of great architectural interest.

Probably the starkest illustration of the early fourteenth-century tower-house is Loch Leven Castle, standing on an island in the loch of the same name. This compact structure (36 feet by 32 feet) rises to five storeys, consisting of a cellar, kitchen, hall, solar and garret. The entrance is directly on to the second floor by means of an outside stair or ladder. The domestic arrangements were extremely spartan, yet one has to admire Loch Leven as a model of economy.

Its modest appearance belies the excellence of the masonry.

By contrast, Threave Castle, set on an island in the River Dee in Kircudbrightshire, is the mighty baronial version of the same theme. Built soon after 1369 by the formidable 3rd Earl of Douglas, Archibald the Grim, its scarred ruin still rises to a height of 70 feet.

Such was the vogue for vertical defence that not even a king could resist its appeal. The first Stewart king, Robert II (1371-90), built the mightiest of tower-houses at Dundonald in Ayrshire, today a ruggedly impressive ruin of commanding stature.

But the most forbidding of Scotland's early tower-houses is surely Hermitage

Hermitage Castle

Castle, surrounded by the bleak moors of Liddesdale in the border country. This is an aberrant type, being a conversion of a manor house which was absorbed into a tower-house of unusual girth with projecting square towers linked by an overhanging parapet. Steeped in romantic associations of the darker sort, Hermitage Castle has a dour and chilling aspect.

A grim austerity characterises the tower-houses of the fourteenth century. These essentially passive structures were as inward-looking as the defensive brochs of a thousand years before. Their basic aim was to repel raids rather than withstand organised sieges. They have to be imagined with a low barmkin wall which offered some protection for their livestock and with fires blazing to dispel the chill of their stone vaults. As the style evolved in later centuries the tower-house became a more commodious and even fanciful work of architecture, but the stark early examples best express the true nature of the genre.

GAZETTEER 4

Abbeys and Priories
1 Arbroath
2 Balmerino
3 Beauly
4 Cambuskenneth
5 Coldingham
6 Crossraguel
7 Dryburgh
8 Dundrennan
9 Dunfermline
10 Glenluce
11 Holyrood
12 Inchcolm
13 Inchmahome
14 Iona
15 Jedburgh
16 Kelso
17 Melrose
18 Oronsay
19 Paisley
20 Pluscarden
21 Restenneth
22 Sweetheart

Cathedrals and Churches
23 Dalmeny Kirk
24 Dunblane Cathedral
25 Dunkeld Cathedral
26 Edrom Norman Arch
27 Elgin Cathedral
28 Glasgow Cathedral
29 Leuchars Parish Church
30 Orphir Church, Orkney
31 St Andrew's Cathedral
32 St Magnus Cathedral, Kirkwall
33 St Magnus Church, Egilsay
34 St Margaret's Chapel, Edinburgh
35 St Rule's Church, St Andrew's

Castles
36 Balvenie
37 Bothwell

38 Caerlaverock
39 Cawdor
40 Craigmillar
41 Cubbie Roo's
42 Dirleton
43 Doune
44 Drum
45 Duart
46 Dundonald
47 Dunnottar
48 Dunstaffnage
49 Dunvegan
50 Hermitage
51 Kildrummy
52 Kisimul
53 Loch Leven
54 Lochranza
55 Mingarry
56 Morton
57 Neidpath
58 Rothesay
59 Skipness
60 Stirling
61 Sween
62 Tantallon
63 Threave
64 Tioram
65 Traquair
66 Turnberry
67 Urquhart

Historic Sites
68 Bannockburn
69 Bruce's Stone, Loch Trool
70 Bruce's Stone, Moss Raploch

Norman Mounds
71 Bass of Inverurie
72 Coulter Motte
73 Doune of Invernochty
74 Mote of Urr
75 Peel of Lumphanan

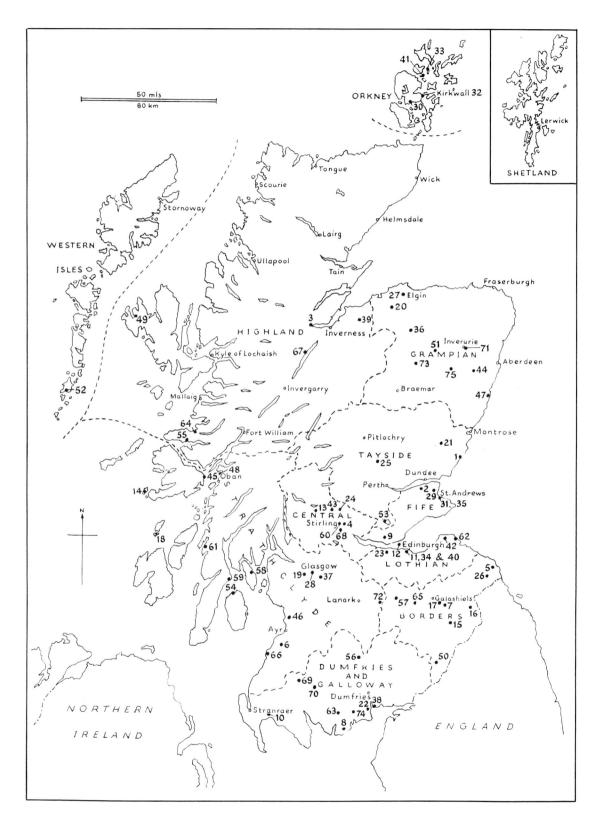

50 mls
80 km

5 The Age of the Royal House of Stewart

The Stewart dynasty played a pivotal rôle in the history of Scotland from the accession of Robert II in 1371 to the defeat of Bonny Prince Charlie at Culloden in 1746. This period witnessed the emergence of Scotland from the Middle Ages into a brief Renaissance, cut short by the Reformation, and finally into modern times. However, things evolved slowly at the beginning of the Stewart era; and in terms of Scotland's cultural and political development, the last fifty years of the House of Stewart represented a doomed enterprise. The failed attempt to reintroduce a Catholic monarchy in a country which had become substantially Protestant, indeed Presbyterian, was out of step with the march of history. Thus it is the fifteenth to seventeenth centuries which provide the essential achievements of the Royal House of Stewart.

The major political landmarks of the period were the acquisition of Orkney and Shetland in 1469; the massacre of the flower of Scottish chivalry by the English at Flodden Field in 1513; the Reformation from the middle of the sixteenth century; the Union of the Crowns in 1603; the Wars of the Covenant in the seventeenth century; and the Treaty of Union in 1707 which united the parliaments of England and Scotland. On the face of it the Scots might appear to have taken over as monarchs of England with the accession of James VI of Scotland as James I of England in 1603, but the underlying reality was a steady advance of English control over Scottish affairs which eventually saw the country reduced to a subordinate rôle as North Britain. On the domestic front, the Stewarts succéeded in their attempts to assert royal authority over baronial ambitions, and the power of the mighty Douglas family was finally broken in 1455. The turbulent Lords of the Isles, who maintained a proud, autonomous lifestyle from their strongholds in the Gaelic west, suffered a grievous setback in 1493 when the Lordship was forfeited to the Stewarts, and in the course of the sixteenth century central government extended into the Hebrides and western regions. There were thus two parallel developments under the Stewarts: the subjugation of the clans by the Scottish monarchy and the steady encroachment on the power of the Scottish monarchy by England.

However, that is to anticipate events which would not have seemed at all apparent at the beginning of the fifteenth century. In 1424, as the thirty-year-old James I of Scots rode north, after eighteen years as a prisoner of the English, to assume control over his rightful kingdom, Scotland was still enshrouded in the chrysalis of the Middle Ages. But James I was a strong man, a stern enforcer of law and order as well as a poet of no mean ability. Through him came the first breeze of the Renaissance to dispel the thick northern mists. He has been hailed as the first true king to rule Scotland since Robert the Bruce, but his handling of the clans was often disdainful. His assassination in 1437 left the six-year-old James II exposed to a world of murderous intrigue. Yet James II managed not only to survive but also to advance royal authority over baronial anarchy. It was he who broke the challenge of the Douglas family, but he met an unfortunately premature end when one of his own cannon exploded at Roxburgh in 1460. The nine-year-old James III proved to be less of a leader but he made his mark as a patron of the arts, especially music. His interest in the sciences of astronomy, medicine and surgery as well as in architecture and interior decoration set the scene for the fuller flow of the Renaissance spirit under his son and successor, the charismatic James IV.

James IV was all of sixteen years of age on his accession in 1488, a considerable advantage in maturity over other Stewart monarchs. He was by all accounts the best loved of the Stewarts. Under him occurred a flourishing of the arts, science and education. With his residence in the palace he had built next to the Abbey of Holyrood, Edinburgh became the permanent capital of the kingdom. Yet the brilliant achievements of this Renaissance prince were tragically cut short by his heroic and futile death in battle against the English at Flodden Field in 1513. The two-year-old James V inherited a throne surrounded by a resurgence of baronial feuding which reached a climax in 1520 at a monstrous and bloody brawl in Edinburgh. Even after his investiture in 1523 James V was held prisoner by his own barons in Edinburgh Castle; he managed to escape in 1528 and fled to the relative safety of Stirling. He eventually established himself as a tough ruler with a merciless streak. Although he isolated himself by his coldness of character, he was a flamboyant patron of architecture and lavished a fortune on his household, promoting splendid improvements to the royal palaces at Falkland, Stirling, Linlithgow and Edinburgh, more than the rest of the Stewart monarchs combined. Yet James V died a disappointed man at the age of only thirty, leaving behind a newly born daughter, who became known as Mary Queen of Scots, and predicting dire things for the House of Stewart.

Until the palatial buildings of the Stewart kings introduced a note of Renaissance style into Scotland the national architecture had been extremely martial in character. Tower-houses studded the land, and from these strongholds the barons and lairds exercised the power of 'pit and gallows' over the local population. The spirit of militarism even influenced ecclesiastical building, and some churches, such as that at Torpichen, assumed an embattled appearance. There was, however, an impressive burst of creativity with the construction of a new religious foundation for secular clergy, known as the collegiate church. But around the middle of the sixteenth century a combination of forces conspired to bring a halt to any architectural achievement and to cause the destruction of many fine buildings of the Middle Ages: in 1544 Henry VIII of England inaugurated his series of raids across the border which devastated towns, castles, abbeys and palaces. The aim of these punitive campaigns was to persuade the Scots to agree to the betrothal of the infant Queen Mary to his son Edward. Henry VIII's acts of terrorism have gone down in history graced with the ironic title of the 'Rough Wooing' – a courtship which was ultimately unsuccessful. As for Mary, the target of the exercise, she was sent to a safe refuge on the island of Inchmahome on the Lake of Menteith before being despatched to France, where she married the Dauphin, the future François II, who died within a year of his coronation.

Meanwhile, events of a more cataclysmic nature had been brewing which would soon bring about from within a complete revolution in Scottish affairs. The burning of Patrick Hamilton in 1528 at St Andrews for his radical beliefs was the first martyrdom of the Reformation in Scotland. That of George Wishart in 1546 had a profound influence on John Knox, the man who was to determine the final character of the triumphant Reformed Church in Scotland along its austere Calvinistic lines. By the time Mary Queen of Scots returned home from France in 1561 to take up her throne the cause of the Scottish Reformation had already been won with the assistance of Elizabeth I of England. With John Knox now preaching in vehement spirit from the pulpit of St Giles in Edinburgh, the presence of the young Catholic queen in the Palace of Holyroodhouse about half a mile away made for one of the most melodramatic confrontations in Scottish history. Fascinating as this was, it represented no more than a sideshow. The short and unhappy reign of Mary turned out to be an historical irrelevance. Although Mary's trail through Scotland is still paved with romantic memories, Knox's Reformation was of a real and enduring significance.

Scotland's destiny was becoming ever more closely embroiled with that of England. James VI, who succeeded to the throne of Scotland in 1567, found himself called to London in 1603 to rule as King of England as well. Thereafter he treated his native Scotland as no more than a distant province and in fact made only one visit north before he died in 1625. In the course of the Civil War in England between Parliamentarians and Royalists, Scotland found itself involved on the side of the rebels, largely as a result of Scottish support for the Presbyterian cause enshrined in the National Covenant of 1638. However, the execution of Charles I in 1649 did much to alienate Scottish sympathies, and the exiled Charles II was invited to accept the crown of Scotland. This prompted an invasion by Cromwell who incorporated Scotland into his short-lived Commonwealth. There are traces of Cromwellian forts, notably at Ayr, Leith, Perth, Inverlochy and Inverness, but none of these fortifications is intact, being overlaid and destroyed by subsequent urban development.

The Restoration of the monarchy in 1660 brought in its wake moves to re-impose the old episcopal system in Scotland. These efforts were intensified after the death of Charles II in 1685 by the overtly Catholic James II, and supporters of the Covenant were brutally repressed. The Presbyterian Reformation was finally established during the reign of William of Orange but the deposition of James II gave birth to the Jacobite movement which aimed to restore the Stewart monarchy. Towards the end of the seventeenth century economic circumstances pushed Scotland inexorably into ever great dependence on England. The accompanying political pressure eventually led to the Treaty of Union of 1707, whereby the Scottish and English parliaments were united at Westminster. Scotland's impressive new Parliament House in Edinburgh, built between 1632 and 1639, served its original purpose for less than a hundred years.

Scottish architecture recovered quickly from the lull during the first half of the sixteenth century and there was a marked resumption of building activity after the Reformation of 1560. With the partial redistribution of church lands and property the lairds and barons were able to indulge their taste for fanciful houses and castles. Even existing strongholds were embellished by a late blossoming of Renaissance-inspired detail such as the remarkable façade in Caerlaverock Castle and the elegant formal garden laid out next to the austere tower of Edzell. The old style of the tower-house was revived and rapidly underwent further development to culminate in the great flowering of the Scottish Baronial style. Merchants were now able to afford houses on a par with the nobility. The castle of Craigievar, the epitome of the genre, was built in 1626 by Master William Forbes, known as 'Danzig Willie' on account of his fortune made in the Baltic trade. The seventeenth century also saw the appearance of some palatial structures on a new quadrangular or courtyard plan, such as Drumlanrig Castle in Dumfriesshire and Sir William Bruce's extension of the Palace of Holyroodhouse

Edzell Castle – a sturdy tower-house acquires a stately garden

between 1671 and 1679 which set the neoclassical fashion for superior building works of the next century.

Less dramatic but more significant in Scotland's overall development at this time was the steady rise of the burghs. The basic 'high street' pattern of the typical burgh applied also to Edinburgh until the end of the eighteenth century. There is a graphic description of Edinburgh as it emerged from the Middle Ages by Fynes Moryson,

Caerlaverock Castle – a Renaissance gem in a medieval setting

writing at the very end of the sixteenth century: 'From the Kings Pallace at the East, the City still riseth higher and higher towards the West, and consists of one broade and very faire street, which is the greatest part and sole ornament thereof, the rest of the side streets and allies being of poore building and inhabited with very poore people . . . .' In 1674 the town council ordained that all new buildings should be of stone and some of the tall tenement blocks of the 'closes' of Edinburgh date back to the end of the seventeenth century. The neat urban scene of today should not obscure the fact that Edinburgh at the time of the Union in 1707 suffered from filthy, overcrowded conditions with a population of over 60,000 crammed into little more than one half of a square mile.

Glasgow had so far given little indication of the meteoric path its development was to follow in the eighteenth and nineteenth centuries. Its population around 1700 is estimated to have amounted to only about 15,000 people, roughly a quarter of Edinburgh's total. In a report to the Convention of Royal Burghs in 1692 Glasgow pleaded that her trade was in such decay that some 500 houses in the town were standing empty. In the city's subsequent dynamic growth most of the mediaeval city was demolished. A town house of 1471, known as Provand's Lordship, is the only building left in Glasgow, with the exception of the cathedral, able to claim any mediaeval origin.

Life in Scotland was, however, still predominantly rural rather than urban, and there was furthermore a marked contrast between the agricultural Lowlands and the as yet untamed wilds of the Highlands. John Major, the historian born around 1569 at Gleghornie near North Berwick, noted:

> One half of Scotland speaks Irish, and all these as well as the Islanders we reckon belong to the Wild Scots. In dress, in the manner of their outward life, and in good morals, for example, these come behind the householding Scots. They live upon others, and follow their own worthless and savage chief in all evil courses sooner than they will pursue an honest industry. They are full of mutual dissensions, and war rather than peace is their normal condition.

Not until the nineteenth century, long after the brutal suppression of the clans, did a more positive if heavily romanticised image of Celtic Scotland come to redress the balance.

The contrast between Highlands and Lowlands was reflected in social and economic aspects. As the burghs evolved into wealthy trading centres so they acquired the benefits of an advanced civilisation. St Andrew's University of 1411 was soon followed by that of Glasgow in 1450 and Aberdeen in 1494. In 1506 Edinburgh received a royal charter to found a College of Surgeons, and in 1508 the city started Scotland's first printing press. At the same time conditions in the north and the west remained primitive. Dionyse Settle recorded a visit to Orkney in 1577: 'Their houses are verie simply built with pibble stone, without any chimneys, the fire being made in the midst thereof. The good man, wife, children, and others of the familie eate and sleepe on the one side of the house and their catell on the other, very beastlie and rudely in respect of civilitie.' The house in question can have been hardly superior in its domestic arrangements to a dwelling of the Iron Age. Similar conditions could still be found in the Highlands even at the end of the nineteenth century.

Yet the most serious weakness of Highland society was neither poverty nor primitivism but the fatal divisions between the clans. The Stewart monarchs managed to consolidate their own authority by consistently exploiting the enmities of the rival clan chiefs. Ironically, the death-knell of both the Royal House of Stewart and of the clans was sounded by the failure of the Jacobite movement on the field of Culloden in 1746. This was to be the final episode of a blood-stained era which had for so long consumed the energies and talents of Scotland in feuds and in wars. The fruits of the Union with England in 1707 were to be slow in coming but within a few years of the defeat of Charles Edward Stewart Edinburgh was one of the leading centres of that great advance in European civilisation known as the Enlightenment.

Haddington House – fine burgh architecture of the early seventeenth century

Tower-houses for all Tastes

The tower-house tradition, which had been launched in the late thirteenth century, had become the dominant form of fortified residence in the fourteenth and continued to flourish for the next two centuries. This marked the birth of a distinctly Scottish national style of architecture which was taken up across a wide spectrum of society from minor lairds to mighty barons. No greater contrast in scope and refinement can be found than between the mighty castle of Borthwick (1430) in Midlothian and the modest Smailholm Tower near Kelso which dates from the early sixteenth century.

Borthwick's massive external appearance is enhanced by the fine ashlar masonry and the closeness of the two projecting wings. Via the main entrance on the first floor there is access to the baronial hall, a magnificent vaulted chamber, which was originally a riot

Smailholm Tower

of colourful decoration with allegorical scenes painted on the plaster. It was only on the first floor that the wings connected *en suite* with the main chamber. The three further storeys are a complex arrangement of rooms at various levels, some within the walls being only accessible via cleverly concealed staircases. Any intruder who managed to gain entry to Borthwick would require considerable local knowledge to avoid becoming hopelessly lost in the stone labyrinth within the fourteen-foot thick walls. A refined defensive device thus dictated the layout of the interior as well as the martial aspect of the exterior, making Borthwick the most sophisticated of tower-houses.

Smailholm Tower of about a century later is a more modest version of the genre; in fact it is no more than a vertical farmhouse rather than a castle proper. Its seven-foot walls of random rubble support a four-storey structure, which consists of a simple stacking of one room above the one below. But the tower itself could only protect the human occupants of Smailholm; the livestock remained vulnerable even within the barmkin wall, and there are several accounts of horses and cattle being carried away by raiders.

Set side by side Smailholm Tower and Borthwick exemplify the tremendously broad acceptance of the tower-house idea in Scotland and provide fine illustrations of the national virtues of economy, cunning and self-reliance in the stubborn defensive thinking which is so typical of this building style.

Courtly Style of the Stewart Monarchs

By the end of the fifteenth century, tower-house building had slumped. Possibly, there were enough 'houses of fence' in Scotland to satisfy the demand; possibly, the triumph of royal authority over the turbulent Douglas barons had improved security in the land. Certainly, the disastrous defeat of the Scottish forces in 1513 at Flodden Field had decimated the nobility on whose patronage the building of castles largely depended. Whatever the exact combination of circumstances, it is a remarkable fact that the baronial contribution to the architectural record of the first half of the sixteenth century was meagre indeed. Yet the Stewart monarchy under James IV and V filled the vacuum with a spate of palatial construction which has become known as the Court School. Their works at Holyrood, Linlithgow, Stirling and Falkland provided a breath of fresh air, a whiff of the European Renaissance, and marked a dramatic departure from the prevailing mood of Scottish domestic architecture with its obdurate insistence on vertical defence.

However, one of the first works commissioned by James IV in 1500 was a defensive type of tower-house with massive corner roundels at Falkland Palace. But under James V Falkland's south range acquired between 1537 and 1542 one of the most uncompromising Renaissance-style façades. This flamboyant display of European fashion was in fact only an exercise in window-dressing for it was simply tacked on to the solidly Gothic range, whose original aspect, complete with buttresses, can be seen on the other side of the building.

Stirling Castle contains behind its Hanoverian battlements some notable examples of the courtly style of the Stewarts. The Great Hall, largely the work of James III but completed by James IV around 1505, is still native in general appearance but the royal palace block adjacent to it, which was completed by James V in 1540, has a wealth of Renaissance-inspired decorative details which disguises the underlying Gothic character. The most remarkable feature of these buildings is the exuberant array of statues standing upon wall shafts of clear Renaissance origin. These figures are a curious amalgam of classical and grotesque, suggesting a meeting of mediaeval and modern ideas. They represent quite the most hybrid architectural *tour de force* in Scotland.

Alone of the great Stewart palaces in Scotland Linlithgow is today a ruin, but an eloquent one indeed, well preserved and dramatically situated in parkland by a loch. The present palace goes back to 1425-35 during the reign of James I but it owes most

Linlithgow Palace

James V's palace block in Stirling Castle

to James IV and James V, who added passages, galleries, stairs and saw the structure evolve into a full quadrangular complex. Apart from the north range, which was rebuilt in 1618-20 during the reign of James VI in the neoclassical manner, the palace of Linlithgow embodies the spirit of the early Stewart style with its blend of Gothic and Renaissance. James V's French Queen, Mary of Guise, said it was the most princely home she had ever seen. Perhaps there was a degree of flattery in her words but by the standards of the day Linlithgow was a royal residence indeed; and it was still grand and impressive despite its subsequent neglect when the Stewart monarchs ruled from London. As early as 1668 there was a report that 'the Palace, which has been werie magnificent is now for the most part ruinous'.

In order to conjure up the former splendour of Linlithgow and the other palaces of the Stewarts we have to imagine the silk and velvet of the upholstery, the rich hangings of damask, tapestries on the wall, gold and silver plate on the oak tables, roaring fires, music and merriment. But for much of the time the palaces would have been empty and bare, for the Stewart monarchs maintained a peripatetic court, proceeding from palace to palace with a huge baggage train which contained both their household and much of their furnishings as well. This mobile lifestyle resulted from the current practice of consuming rents in kind, but partly for health reasons since the primitive sanitary arrangements could not cope for long with such large numbers of people.

Of the original palace at Holyrood, begun

by James IV, only a tower remains and this has been totally absorbed into the 1671 rebuilding in the neoclassical manner com-missioned by Charles II. Thus it is the palaces of Falkland, Stirling and Linlithgow which in almost equal proportion exemplify

Linlithgow Palace

the early Stewart architectural style. Yet the initiative of the Court School in introducing Renaissance ideas was not taken up immediately by the Scottish nobility. Security was still more important than comfort and elegance. In the second half of the sixteenth century there was a marked renewal of interest in the tower-house; and it was at this time that it embarked on its final and grandest phase.

Falkland Palace

129

Collegiate Churches

The Early Middle Ages in Scotland had witnessed the flowering of the glorious Anglo-Norman abbeys and cathedrals. The fifteenth century saw a remarkable shift in emphasis towards more modest acts of piety in the form of smaller ecclesiastical foundations. This was the great era of the parish church in Scotland, but also, more significantly, that of the collegiate church. The so-called 'colleges' of secular (i.e. non-monastic) clergy were founded by men of wealth and power, partly perhaps as an aversion to the luxury of the great monasteries which was beginning to attract criticism. However, the endowment of a collegiate church was not entirely altruistic for its chief task was to sing masses and chant prayers for the salvation of the benefactor and his noble family.

A characteristic specimen of the genre is Dunglass Collegiate Church in East Lothian, where an older chapel dedicated to the Virgin Mary was converted into its present form in the 1440s by Sir Alexander Hume and raised to collegiate status in 1450. There is an impressive quality to this austere structure of fine yellow sandstone ashlar, which has survived the depredations of war and use as a stable with its vaulted roof of stone intact. The overall severity of its

The 'Apprentice Pillar', Rosslyn Chapel

aspect enhances the small amount of carved detail such as the delicate sedilia to good effect and gives the church a solid Scottish character, a model of economy and sobriety.

Such qualities, however, were not to define the type. In fact, the most renowned of Scotland's collegiate churches, Rosslyn Chapel in Midlothian, is the most flamboyantly ornate building imaginable. Its exuberant and fanciful stone carvings are without parallel in Europe. This jewel was constructed over a period of forty years from

1446 onwards, being dedicated as the Collegiate Church of St Matthew in 1450 on completion of the foundations. Yet only a part of the founder Sir William St Clair's grandiose scheme was carried out prior to his death in 1484 and the nave was never built.

But even incomplete, Rosslyn Chapel is a breathtaking experience of the vitality and virtuosity of the mediaeval mason's craft. The abundance of carvings amounts to no less than a picture book in stone of predominantly biblical scenes such as the expulsion from the Garden of Eden, the tales of Samson and Isaac, the Crucifixion, the Apostles and four martyrs each carrying the instrument of his martyrdom. There are unique renderings of the Dance of Death, a favourite mediaeval subject, as well as allegorical portrayals such as the Seven Virtuous Acts and the Seven Deadly Sins. Decorative carvings adorn every available space. The beams and rib vaults are a riot of geometrical foliage patterns which inspired an ecstatic diary note by Dorothy Wordsworth and a

fine poem by her brother William on the occasion of their visit to Rosslyn in 1803.

The catalogue of Rosslyn's carvings is endless. Alongside the biblical are human portrayals of common folk and gentry. There are dragons, and even an angel playing the bagpipes. The undisputed centrepiece is the so-called Apprentice Pillar, a most accomplished work consisting of a spiral of four strands of foliage twisting around the column. Legend has it that the jealous master mason killed his more gifted apprentice by a blow of his mallet. Was ever such artistry so cruelly rewarded?

Tomb of the Stewart Princess Margaret in Lincluden Abbey

Lincluden Abbey at Dumfries

A further variation on the theme of the collegiate church can be seen at Lincluden in Dumfriesshire. This new foundation of Archibald the Grim in 1389 was actually built by his successor the 4th Earl of Douglas between 1409 and 1424. At the heart of this church of red Permian sandstone, which has been described as 'a virginal piece of purest Decorated Gothic', is the tomb of the Earl's wife the Princess Margaret, daughter of Robert III. This shrine with its wealth of heraldic blazonry is an integral part of the chancel and the only surviving tomb of the Stewarts in Scotland. Lincluden, although hard-pressed by the modern sprawl of Dumfries, still holds its own as one of the most picturesque ruins in Scotland, thanks to its riverside location next to the outline of a mediaeval garden watched over by the grass-covered hump of a Norman motte.

Lincluden, Rosslyn and Dunglass are but three notable examples of the proliferation of collegiate churches in the fifteenth century. Each has a deeply individual style which represents a distinctly Scottish approach to ecclesiastical architecture at a time when the country was cut off by the wars with England from its customary sources of inspiration.

133

The Heritage of John Knox

A measure of the stature of the great Reformer John Knox can be conveyed by one of the briefest of testimonials, that of Thomas Carlyle in 1840: 'The one Scotchman to whom of all others, his country and the world owe a debt.' Yet there is nothing in Scotland amounting to a Knox cult, as there is for example a Burns cult, an idea that would in any case have been anathema to Knox himself. But there is no shortage of statues to the great Reformer. Edinburgh possesses two fine full-length bronze likenesses, one in the Cathedral of St Giles, and the other in the courtyard of the General Assembly. Of lesser fame is the more prominent statue of Knox high on a column on the hill occupied by the Glasgow Necropolis. The merchants of the city, who subscribed to the erection of the monument in 1825, saw fit to have inscribed on the base of the column their appreciation of the true heritage of John Knox: 'The Reformation produced a revolution in the sentiments of mankind, the greatest as well as the most beneficial that has happened since the publication of Christianity.'

Apart from such memorials, relatively little remains to serve as a reminder of the actual life of the man. He was born in the burgh of Haddington around 1514 but there is no Knox birthplace, and the John Knox House in Edinburgh's Royal Mile, which comes closest to being a Knox shrine, has no authenticated association with the man. Thus it is the scenes of the man's career which most evoke his memory, notably St Giles in Edinburgh where he preached many of his vehement sermons. The castle at St Andrews was the focal point of an abortive uprising after the burning of the Reformer George Wishart in 1546. Knox then spent nineteen months as a galley slave following his capture by the French.

St John's Church in Perth was the scene of Knox's most famous sermon on 11 May 1559, which was such a fiery condemnation of the evils of idolatry that it sparked off a wave of iconoclasm. The scattered ruins of the nearby Abbey of Scone can be seen as a direct result of Knox's tirade; but the Reformation was not such a destructive force as is sometimes imagined. Many of Scotland's mediaeval abbeys and priories were already suffering from neglect, and it was their subsequent abandonment after the Reformation rather than wanton destruction which brought about their steady decay and final ruin.

Possibly the most potent evocation of the spirit of John Knox, as well as his most lasting memorial, was the new generation of post-Reformation churches. There was a radical reorientation inside the church away from the soaring vistas of Gothic arches and high altars towards the layout known as auditory, where the preacher's pulpit became the focal point of the church service and of the architecture. One of the first and finest surviving examples of the new mode is Burntisland Parish Church in Fife, originally built between 1592 and 1595. The spirit of Knox also lives on in countless modest country churches in Scotland, whose austerity commands respect. A fine specimen of the type is the tiny kirk at Glenbuchat which still retains its eighteenth-century interior of wooden stalls and cobbled aisles. Such simple 'preaching boxes', as they have been called, represent a return to the basic rectangular form of the Celtic churches which existed in Scotland before the introduction of the sophisticated Anglo-Norman style in the twelfth century. In this sense Knox may be credited not only with a spiritual but also an architectural revolution in Scotland.

Statue of John Knox in the courtyard of the General Assembly, Edinburgh

The Trail of Mary Queen of Scots

Unlike her father James V, Mary was unable during her brief and unhappy reign to devote much of her energies to anything as enduring as architectural works. Nevertheless the romantic aura surrounding Mary is so strong and bright that her name lives on in the places which mark the stages of her itinerant years in Scotland. Owing to the turbulent nature of her destiny there are many places where she paused but briefly, like some gorgeous butterfly on its erratic course: a few days hunting at Blair, a night at Traquair with Darnley, and at Borthwick with Bothwell. But there are four main locations in the drama of Mary Queen of Scots which sum up the tragedy of her reign.

The tiny island of Inchmahome in the Lake of Menteith was Mary's first taste of the life of refuge which later became her lot. She was taken there as an infant by her mother to escape Henry VIII's punitive military campaign, the 'Rough Wooing' by which the English monarch hoped to persuade the Scots to agree to the betrothal of Mary to his sickly son Edward. The ruins of Inchmahome Priory where Mary stayed as a child may be seen as an early omen of her future imprisonment on another tiny Scottish island.

The royal apartments in the old part of Holyroodhouse are indelibly linked with the brutal assassination of Mary's Italian secretary David Riccio in 1566 by her second husband Darnley and others. It was also at Holyrood that Mary had her four historic confrontations with John Knox, whose bullying method of argument reduced the young queen to tears. The struggle between palace and pulpit, as symbolised by Holyroodhouse and St Giles, was little more than a rearguard action, for the cause of the Reformation in Scotland had already been won in 1560 while Mary was still in France.

The Mary Queen of Scots House in

Jedburgh recalls the impetuous and romantic nature of the lady. It was from here that Mary set out on her almost fatal twelve-mile ride across the bleak moors to visit the ailing Bothwell at Hermitage Castle. At one point she fell from her horse at a spot now called The Queen's Mire and was taken to a humble farmhouse for her clothes to be dried and repaired. The French watch that she lost on that occasion is now on display in the house at Jedburgh where she subsequently recuperated. The story goes that the elegant timepiece was pushed back to the surface inadvertently by an unsuspecting

Island of Inchmahome, Lake of Menteith

mole, and was rediscovered in 1817.

One of the last stages of Mary's bitter progress through Scotland was the island castle of Loch Leven where she was held prisoner for ten months at the time she abdicated in favour of her son who was crowned James VI. Her escape from this Scottish prison was but the prelude to Mary's mistaken flight to England, where she was to endure nineteen more wearisome years of confinement before meeting the executioner's axe at Fotheringay in 1587. Her last night on Scottish soil was spent at the beautiful Cistercian abbey of Dundrennan close to the Solway Firth whence she set sail.

Mary's historical destiny was that of a romantic, caught up in a great tide of events in which she could never hope to steer her own course. Yet this Catholic queen of a vigorously Protestant country has been overwhelmingly rehabilitated as a national heroine in Scotland's epic struggle with England, alongside Wallace and Bruce. It is fair to say that Mary achieved more in the manner of her death by the hand of the English Queen Elizabeth than by anything accomplished during her lifetime.

Twilight Era of the Lords of the Isles

In St Clement's Church at Rodel on the southern tip of the island of Harris in the Outer Hebrides is one of the most evocative of ancient monuments in Scotland. The elaborately carved grave-slab and tomb of Alasdair Crottach, 8th Chief of the MacLeods of Dunvegan and Harris, is a potent reminder of the erstwhile autonomy of the Hebridean clans who managed to resist the authority of the Scottish monarchy until the very end of the fifteenth century. The effigy of the MacLeod Chief is a masterpiece of carving in black schist set beneath an arch. The wall and the arch itself are decorated with a number of magnificently carved panels which illustrate a touching blend of heavenly and earthly subjects. On either side of the central group comprising the Virgin and Child flanked by a bishop and St Clement we see a mediaeval castle and a galley under sail, the two poles of an island chief's power, denoting supremacy on the waters and an impregnable stronghold on the land. It is not without irony that this most sumptuous

Tomb of Alasdair Crottach of Dunvegan in St Clement's Church, Rodel, Harris

memorial was constructed in 1528, thirty-five years after the forfeiture of the Lordship of the Isles in 1493 to James IV.

The Lordship was a curious amalgam of Celtic and Nordic elements which emerged from the old Hebridean dominion of the Kings of Norway. Basically Gaelic in culture, the Lords of the Isles took pride in an ancestry which reached back via Somerled and the Dalriadic line to the most remote

Irish antiquity with Conn of the Hundred Battles, High King of Tara. In its heyday the Lordship of the Isles commanded all of the Hebrides and much of the Western Highlands as well; this last bastion of Gaeldom in Scotland survived until around the middle of the fifteenth century. The art of the Lords of the Isles forms one of the most moving chapters of Scotland's cultural heritage. This tough breed of fighters and sea-raiders has

Chieftain's tomb in St Clement's Church, Rodel, Harris

139

bequeathed a series of beautifully fashioned grave-slabs as a most poignant memory of their days of glory. These recumbent effigies combine the fierce equipment of the warrior, such as pointed helmets, hoods of mail, leather shields and the enormous two-handed claymores, with the delicacy of finely carved natural motifs and elements from Christian mythology. The realistic portrayals of their warships speak of the Norse strain in their blood and of their navigational skills.

The great flowering of this sculpture occurred under the influence of Irish masons settled mainly in Iona. Examples of this unique cultural heritage from all over the scattered territory of the Lords of the Isles have been gathered together in a number of small collections such as those in Iona, Oronsay Priory, Saddell Abbey, Kilmartin, Kilberry and Kilmory Knap in Kintyre. These grave-slabs, some well preserved and others eroded by the weather or damaged by vandalism, offer a more realistic picture of life at the time than even the ruins of the castles of the western seaboard such as Tioram, Mingarry and Dunollie or the renovated Hebridean strongholds of Dunvegan on Skye, Duart on Mull, and

Effigies of Highland chieftains at Kilmory Knap, Argyll

Kisimul on Barra. An island in Loch Finlaggan on Islay was the administrative centre where the Council of the Lordship used to meet, but this historic site does not convey any sense of the authority or splendour of the Lordship.

It is now nearly five hundred years since the last Lord of the Isles died in 1503 in quite miserable circumstances in a modest lodging house in Dundee but memories of the Lordship have been revived in recent years by the MacDonalds who claim descent from Somerled himself. In the words of the old Celtic bard: 'It is no joy without Clan Donald. It is no strength to be without them.'

Grave-slabs at Kilmory Knap, Argyll

The Rise of the Burghs

Many of Scotland's burghs go back to the twelfth century, notably to the reign of David I, whose far-sighted policy of urban development was to bear fruit throughout the mediaeval period. Although the earliest houses of the burghs have long since disappeared, due to the perishable nature of their building material as well as to subsequent redevelopment in the course of the centuries, these first exercises in Scottish town-planning have left an indelible mark on today's burghs which have, until the end of the seventeenth century, followed the original twelfth-century plan.

This can still be easily discerned in towns throughout Scotland as a high street, or sometimes two in parallel, running from the castle to the kirk, the twin poles of early mediaeval times. Giving off the high street were a series of narrow alleys, closes or vennels at right angles where houses were packed tightly together regardless of the risks of fire and disease. For centuries the

Scottish burghs remained huddled within the protection of their walls so that vertical housing was the only way to accommodate the increase in population. The focal points of the burgh were the tolbooth, which served as both civic centre and jail, and the mercat cross, which was the symbol of the burgh's jurisdiction as well as the site of its market place. At Crail in Fife there is a fine example of a tolbooth which dates back to around 1600, and Prestonpans in East Lothian still retains its original mercat cross of 1617 in the exact position it first occupied more than three hundred and fifty years ago.

As the burghs became more prosperous, so stone replaced timber in the fifteenth century, and it is from this time that the oldest examples of burgh architecture originate. Provand's Lordship in Glasgow of 1471 is recognised as the oldest town-dwelling in Scotland, just earlier than the John Knox House in Edinburgh of 1490 with its wooden front on a structure of stone which was characteristic of its time. There are many interesting descriptions of the aspect of mediaeval Edinburgh and most stress the contrast between the majestic High Street and the insalubrious vennels that gave off it. One must imagine a colourful, crowded, noisy scene but not forget the pungent smell of garbage and raw sewage that lay in the streets of the city.

If one is to believe a description of 1661 of Aberdeen by the cartographer Gordon of Rothiemay then conditions of urban life were markedly better outside the capital: 'The buildings of the toune are of stone and lyme, rigged above, covered with slaits, mostlie of three or four stories high, some of them higher. The streets are all neatlie paved with flint stone . . . . The dwelling houses are cleanlie and bewtifull and neat, both within and without, and the syde that looks to the street, mostlie adorned with galleries of timber . . . . Many houses have their gardings and orcheyards adjoyning; every garding has its posterne, and thes are planted with all sorts of trees which the climat will suffer to grow; so that the quholl

An Edinburgh close, off the High Street

toune, to such as draw neer it . . . looks as if it stood in a garding or little wood.' Two notable survivors of this comely picture of Aberdeen are Provost Ross's House of 1594 and Provost Skene's House, whose title deeds go back to 1545 but whose present structure is essentially an outstanding example of seventeenth-century Scottish domestic architecture. Its fine interiors, and especially the painted ceilings, show the growing refinement of burghal life which was the reward of success in trade.

Whereas Scotland's larger cities can only provide isolated examples of burgh architecture there are a few smaller towns which have conserved more extensive areas of historic interest. Culross in Fife has the most perfect assemblage of typical burgh housing from the seventeenth century onwards. Grouped around the cobbled streets

Provost Ross's House, Aberdeen

which lead off from the mercat cross are rows of neat dwellings with red pantiles, crow-stepped gables and white harling. The prosperity of Culross in the sixteenth and seventeenth centuries came largely from a clever exploitation of the local coal seams under the direction of Sir George Bruce who took over the colliery in 1575. The 'Palace' of Culross is the fine mansion constructed by Sir George, a notable example of the type of residence favoured by an industrial magnate at the end of the sixteenth century. Painted ceilings and wall panels are once again a prominent feature.

Just a few years prior to the death of Sir George Bruce in his palatial home in Culross a certain Thomas Gledstanes acquired in 1617 a property on Edinburgh's High Street which he proceeded to rebuild and extend over the next three years. Today known as Gladstone's Land the house is a noteworthy surviving example of Edinburgh's older façades. Its narrow frontage and high elevation show to a remarkable degree the type of vertical tenement which became the hallmark of the city and remained the basic housing form for rich and poor alike until the stately Georgian New Town was developed

The market-place at Culross

at the end of the eighteenth century. Many wealthy folk occupied only a couple of rooms on one floor, having but the barest essential items of furniture. When Edinburgh was finally able to expand, the people of substance abandoned the mediaeval burgh, leaving behind an impoverishment which still haunts the closes of the old city.

Final Flourish of the Tower-house

Whereas sixteenth-century England had turned its back on castles as such and embarked instead on its grand spell of Elizabethan domestic architecture, there was a markedly different response in Scotland at the same time. Here the continuing insecurity in the land ensured that the tower-house lived on as the basic fortified residence of lairds and barons. In fact there was a positive boom in the construction of new tower-houses in the years following the Reformation as monies which had previously been lavished on religious endowments now became available for secular works. The process was accelerated further as private landowners acquired the property of the Church. During the half-century from 1570 to 1620 the movement surged to a climax. Then there was a decline in the 1630s, and finally a sudden halt in building activity as the turmoil of the Civil War in England spilled over into Scotland following the Covenant of 1637.

This new generation of tower-houses shows a continuing obsession with defence but there is equally a great effort to increase

Menzies Castle

the domestic comfort. The addition of extra wings, or jambs, provided not only more accommodation but also allowed the occupants of the tower-house to cover all sides of their refuge with fire arms, thus discouraging would-be aggressors. At first the extra wing added to one of the corners of the main block formed what is known as the L-plan. The next step was the provision of towers at diagonally opposite corners to create the Z-plan. A fine early but mature example of the Z-plan is Castle Menzies in Perthshire, which dates from 1571 to 1577. It was in rather dilapidated condition when it was taken over by the Menzies Clan Society in 1974 and has been well restored to give an idea of the changing styles of domestic life within a Scottish tower-house.

Claypotts Castle on the outskirts of Dundee, dating from 1569 to 1588, is extremely well preserved, although it has lost all its original ancillary structures and now stands somewhat unhappily surrounded by a group of neat suburban houses. The curious feature at Claypotts is the way a rectangular room has been placed on the top of the circular towers which have been positioned at diagonally opposite corners of the square central tower to form the characteristic Z-plan. There are menacing shot-holes at ground-floor level, one of which is cunningly concealed in the back of the kitchen fire-place.

Such tower-houses as Claypotts and Menzies are satisfying works which do not aspire to artistic heights; but there are several nobler embodiments of the tower tradition such as Glamis, Crathes and Craigievar which merit serious architectural acclaim. Of these, Craigievar demonstrates to the fullest how the original provision for defence had gradually been transmuted into motifs of purely aesthetic significance. Yet the exterior of the house remained essentially true to the tower-house idea, with the lower portion of the wall remaining uncompromisingly blank; and it was only at wall-head level that the architect-mason gave full rein to his decorative impulses. Mock cannons pose as water spouts but no one can really be fooled by the device. Instead of martial strength the overall impression of Craigievar is of graceful gathered power: that of a gymnast or a wrestler rather than that of a mail-clad knight.

The exquisite plaster ceilings of Craigievar, which date back to the original construction of the castle in 1626, reveal a growing concern for ornamentation. This is also evident in the magnificent painted wooden

Craigievar Castle

ceilings at Crathes Castle. Similar colourful and skilfully drawn interiors were a standard feature of lairdly residences in Scotland from the sixteenth century; in some cases the hand of Italian artists can be detected, notably at Kinneil House near Bo'ness.

It is a curious fact that one of the last tower-houses of note to be constructed in Scotland, that of Scotstarvit in Fife of 1627, is a complete regression to the austerity of previous centuries which denied any scope for artistic embellishment. Just fifty years later conditions had changed so much as to mark the end of the tower tradition. In 1677 the Earl of Strathmore, referring to his own strongholds of Huntly and Glamis, commented: 'such houses truly are quite out of fashion, as feuds are . . . the country being generally more civilised that it was of ancient times.'

Glamis Castle

Renaissance Influences

At the same time that the Scottish tower-house was launched on its final and grandest phase so too the style, which has come to be known as Scottish Baronial, was adding a lighter touch with a variety of ornate decorative devices directly inspired by the Renaissance in Europe. There was a tremendous contrast between the home-grown austerity and the fanciful architectural fashions which began to make an appearance

Oriel windows of Huntly Castle

in the second half of the sixteenth century.

The new ideas were applied equally to existing structures as they were to new projects. Thus we see at Crichton Castle one of the most remarkable architectural oddities in Scotland. Here the original stark fourteenth-century tower has become part of a quadrangular complex, one side of which has been covered with an amazing façade of diamond-headed masonry. This exotic work, commissioned by Lord Bothwell shortly after his return from Italy, was

The 'diamond' façade of Crichton Castle

Garden of Edzell Castle

occupants of Scottish castles may be seen in the creation of formal walled gardens. Edzell Castle's 'pleasance' of 1604 is the supreme example in Scotland of its period of a Renaissance-style garden. The proud motto of the Glenesk Lindsays, *'Dum Spiro Spero'* (While I Breathe I Hope), is spelled out in the shape of the hedge. There is a wealth of heraldry and symbolism adorning the walls of the 'pleasance', some subjects directly inspired by German engravings; and the

almost certainly inspired by a visit to the famous Palazzo dei Diamanti in Ferrara.

The reconstruction of Huntly Castle by the first Marquis between 1599 and 1606 owed much to French antecedents. Its splendid range of oriel windows along the upper storey of the south front has obviously been inspired by the example of Blois. Huntly also possesses the most magnificent heraldic doorway in Britain, as well as some richly carved fireplaces bearing the coats of arms and medallion portraits of the 1st Marquis of Huntly George Gordon and his lady Henrietta Stewart.

A similar sense of a cosmetic rather than a martial conversion pervades the works at Tolquhon Castle commissioned by the seventh laird William Forbes which were carried out between 1584 and 1589. Here a spacious courtyard residence replaced a cramped early mediaeval tower. Fanciful gun-loops and elaborate armorial panels proclaim a feudal display of pride rather than any serious military purpose.

Another sign of the trend towards a more elegant and comfortable way of life for the foundations of a bath-house are further testimony to the remarkably civilised environment created by Sir David Lindsay, Lord of Edzell at the beginning of the seventeenth century. Even in its present state of ruin Edzell Castle is a site of great beauty and peace.

Contemporary with Edzell is the Earl's Palace at Kirkwall on Orkney, which is generally acclaimed as Scotland's finest example of an Elizabethan Renaissance-style

Earl's Palace, Kirkwall, Orkney

building. Although the full scheme was never completed, enough stands to indicate the harmonious nature of the original plan with its refined detailing and elegant use of oriel and bay windows. It is strange that this most mature and accomplished cross between a palace and a castle was the work of such a notorious tyrant as Earl Patrick Stewart. It is worth noting that Orkney demonstrates once again that in matters of architectural style it was by no means as peripheral to the mainstream of development as its geographical location might suggest.

One of the last and most surprising works of Renaissance character in Scotland prior to the strife of the Civil War was the remarkable façade commissioned by the Earl of Nithsdale in 1634 to provide an elegant veneer to the courtyard of his mighty early mediaeval castle of Caerlaverock; we find here, within the triple protection of mound, moat and curtain wall, a charming architectural jewel.

The last great Renaissance-style building in Scotland, George Heriot's Hospital in Edinburgh, was commenced in 1627 but the work was interrupted by the Civil War and

Renaissance façade at Caerlaverock Castle

George Heriot's, Edinburgh

did not see completion until 1650. Both chronologically as well as stylistically George Heriot's serves as a bridge between the Renaissance fashions of the first half of the seventeenth century and the full-bodied neoclassical style which followed the Restoration of Charles II in 1660. Its formal layout around a quadrangle points unmistakably to the courtyards of Drumlanrig and Holyroodhouse, but the treatment of the buildings shows an eclectic assemblage of motifs and an underlying Scottishness in the use of elements from the turreted tower-houses of the past. Still in daily use as a school in the historic centre of old Edinburgh beneath the Castle Rock, George Heriot's Hospital is perhaps the last great building in the city prior to the neoclassical revolution pioneered by Sir William Bruce in the 1670s.

Palace of Holyroodhouse, Edinburgh

Dawn of the Neoclassical Age

Following the turbulent years of the Civil War, the Restoration of Charles II in 1660 heralded a new era in more ways than one. In terms of Scotland's architectural development it marked a clear departure from the piecemeal acceptance of Renaissance ideas. What emerged instead was a complete application of the formal classical style of building.

The extension of the Palace of Holyroodhouse which was commenced in 1671 under the direction of Sir William Bruce was the point of departure of the neoclassical movement. The severe façades of the courtyard of the palace, where the Doric, Ionic and Corinthian orders are arrayed with an elegant precision, provided Scotland with its first major example of the style which, a little over a century later, was to earn Edinburgh the popular title of the 'Athens of the North'. It is interesting to note at Holyroodhouse how the outward appearance of the old tower-house was duplicated and so assimilated within a symmetrical front which almost totally disguises its origins. This triumphant resumption of royal patronage of architecture in Scotland some one hundred and thirty years after the death of James V in 1542 was also a clear sign of the grander aspirations of the House of Stewart which now reigned over England as well as Scotland.

The more regal tone of the neoclassical age also found its expression in the formal garden so beloved of France's 'Sun King' Louis XIV. It is thought that it was Sir William Bruce, the architect of Holyrood-

The Great Garden of Pitmedden

house, who brought back to Scotland from his travels in France the basic idea of the noble gardens at Versailles and Vaux-le-Vicomte created by Le Nôtre. Almost certainly, the garden of Sir William Bruce's house at Kinross was influenced by the courtly fashion of France. It seems likely that the same influence was at work in the Great Garden created in 1675 for Sir Alexander Seton at Pitmedden in Aberdeenshire. This spectacular formal garden has been lovingly recreated in recent years under the auspices of the National Trust for Scotland. Three of the four designs for the rectangular parterres were taken from Gordon of Rothiemay's drawings of the garden of the Palace of Holyroodhouse. A terrace overlooks this grand floral compo-

sition, laid out between expanses of smooth green lawn with rows of precisely aligned hedges; and a graceful fountain of sculptured stones is the focal point of the ensemble.

Probably the most flamboyant example of the neoclassical style in architecture in Scotland is the stately home of Drumlanrig Castle in Dumfriesshire built by William Douglas, 1st Duke of Queensberry, between 1679 and 1691 on a former stronghold going back to the fourteenth century. This was Scotland's first truly palatial noble residence on a par with the princely homes of the great English nobles. Although the general impression is of an overwhelmingly classical structure, the exuberance of the carvings in the gentle pink sandstone of Drumlanrig does betray the enthusiastic hand of a native

Drumlanrig Castle

mason-architect. Once again the name of Sir William Bruce crops up but his association with Drumlanrig was restricted to earlier plans to extend the old castle. Unfortunately, the name of the architect responsible for this great private palace, which has been hailed as perhaps the last of a national style in Scotland, remains unknown. Despite the anonymity of its creator Drumlanrig is the most eloquent expression of neoclassical architecture in Scotland prior to the Union with England in 1707.

GAZETTEER 5

Burgh Architecture
1 Argyll's Lodging, Stirling
2 Crail Tolbooth
3 Culross
4 Dunkeld Little Houses
5 Gladstone's Land, Edinburgh
6 Huntly House, Edinburgh
7 John Knox House, Edinburgh
8 Lady Stair's House, Edinburgh
9 Mar's Wark, Stirling
10 Mary Queen of Scots House, Jedburgh
11 Provand's Lordship, Glasgow
12 Provost Ross's, Aberdeen
13 Provost Skene's, Aberdeen

Carvings
14 Iona
15 Kilberry
16 Kilmartin
17 Kilmory Knap
18 Merkland Cross
19 Oronsay Priory
20 Saddell Abbey

Castles
21 Blackness
22 Blair
23 Borthwick
24 Caerlaverock (façade)
25 Campbell
26 Claypotts
27 Craigievar
28 Crathes
29 Crichton (façade)
30 Drumlanrig
31 Earl's Palace, Birsay
32 Earl's Palace, Kirkwall
33 Elcho
34 Fraser
35 Glamis
36 Greenknowe
37 House of the Binns
38 Huntly

39 Kellie
40 Lennoxlove House
41 Menzies
42 Muness
43 Noltland
44 Scalloway
45 Scotstarvit
46 Smailholm
47 Tolquhon
48 Thirlestane

Cathedrals and Churches
49 Burntisland Parish Church
50 Dunglass Collegiate Church
51 High Kirk of St Giles, Edinburgh
52 Lincluden College, Dumfries
53 Rosslyn Chapel
54 St Clement's Church, Rodel
55 St John's Church, Perth
56 St Mary's Church, Haddington
57 St Michael's Church, Linlithgow
58 St Machar's Cathedral, Old Aberdeen
59 Seton Collegiate Church

Educational Institutions
60 George Heriot's Hospital, Edinburgh
61 King's College, Old Aberdeen
62 St Andrews University

Gardens
63 Edzell
64 Pitmedden

Historic Sites
65 Glencoe
66 Pass of Killiecrankie

Royal Palaces
67 Falkland
68 Holyroodhouse
69 Linlithgow
70 Stirling

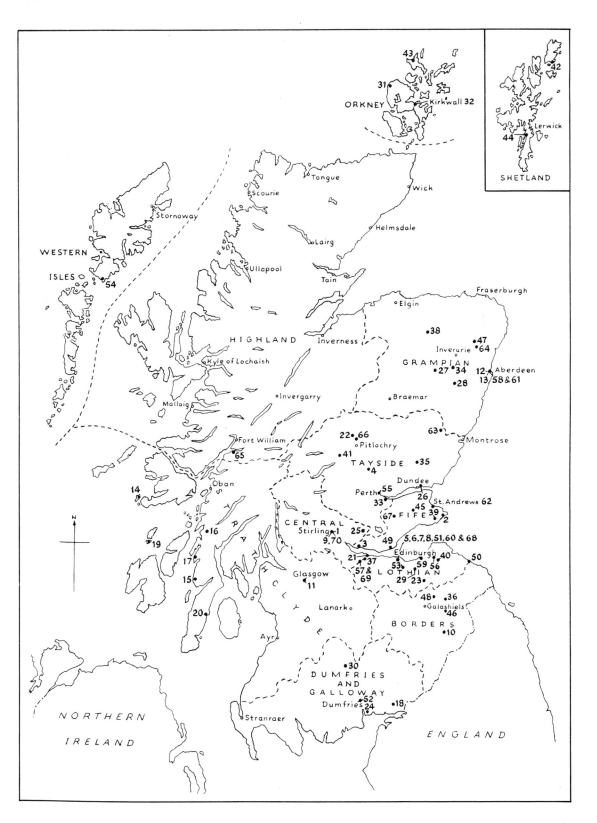

43

31

ORKNEY   •Kirkwall 32

42

Lerwick

44

SHETLAND

•Tongue   •Wick

•Scourie

Stornoway

•Helmsdale

WESTERN

•Lairg

ISLES   o

•54

Ullapool   •Tain

HIGHLAND   Inverness

Fraserburgh

•Elgin

•38   •47

Inverurie •64

Kyle of Lochaish   GRAMPIAN

•27 •34   12•Aberdeen

•Invergarry   •Braemar   •28   13,58&61

Mallaig

22•66   •63   •Montrose

Fort William   •Pitlochry

•65   •41

TAYSIDE   •35

14   •4

Oban   •Dundee

55

Perth•   26   St.Andrews 62

33•   •45

67• FIFE 39

•16   •2

19   CENTRAL   25•   49   5,6,7,8,51,60 & 68

Stirling▲1   •3   •Edinburgh 40   •50

17   9,70   21• •37   53• 59 56

15   •57 & 69   LOTHIAN

Glasgow   29 23

11   48• •36

20   Lanark•   •Galashiels

Ayr•   BORDERS   •46

•10

•30

DUMFRIES

AND

GALLOWAY

•52

Dumfries•24   •18

Stranraer•

NORTHERN

IRELAND   ENGLAND

N

6 Scottish Renaissance

The period that elapsed between the Treaty of Union of 1707 and the accession of Queen Victoria in 1837 might be measured as a brief interlude in the long history of Scotland, but these years witnessed the most dramatic transformation of Scottish life, of Scottish fortunes and indeed of the physical appearance of Scotland itself. In addition to the Industrial Revolution, which swept like a whirlwind through the whole of Britain, there occurred in Scotland a number of other revolutions – in agriculture, architecture, urban development, trade, transport and communications as well as in the social and intellectual domains – as the country gradually recovered from the economic failure of its humiliating colonial venture at Darien and sought to assert itself in the unequal Union with England.

The underlying reasons for the abandonment of Scottish sovereignty were basically commercial, and there was no great feeling of political reconciliation between the countries that had opposed one another for so long. However, the economic benefits of the Union were slow in coming; indeed the British parliament seemed to make a point of penalising Scotland rather than promoting her interests. The Lord Treasurer answering a question, from one of the forty-five MPs sent to represent Scotland at Westminster, concerning a proposed duty on the export of linen retorted: 'Have we not bought the Scots, and a right to tax them too?' And the Speaker stated arrogantly to the Commons that the English had 'catcht Scotland and would keep her fast'.

Against this background of political stalemate the crippling poverty of Scotland added to the sense of national shame, and it was not surprising that there was some support for the Jacobite risings of 1715 and 1719 which aimed to restore the Stewart monarchy in the person of the 'Old Pretender', the would-be James VIII of Scotland and James III of England. In the aftermath of these two failed risings the Hanoverian rulers moved with some urgency to disarm the clans and to pacify the Highlands. The network of forts and garrisons linked by the military roads of General George Wade appeared for a while to underpin the dominance of the forces of law and order, but when Prince Charles Edward Stewart landed with a small band of followers in 1745 to claim the throne on behalf of his father, the British hold on the Highlands turned out to be as tenuous as that of previous occupiers of this rugged wilderness since the time of Julius Agricola. Yet the '45 rising petered out and eventually met its end at Culloden on 16 April 1746; the Highlanders who had been so effective in minor engagements were no match in a pitched battle for the superior forces of a professional army. The site of the defeat at Culloden, which is now cared for as a national shrine, saw the final burial of Scottish hopes for an independent state of their own. The Hanoverian stranglehold on the country was confirmed by the huge garrison at Fort George near Inverness and new fortifications at Dumbarton, Stirling and Edinburgh.

Fireplace at Hopetoun House

Ironically, Culloden marked a positive turning point in Scotland's fortunes. Once the threat of a Jacobite invasion was removed, security was immediately improved and tensions relaxed; energies could now be turned wholly to the challenge of economic growth and development. There was rapid progress across a wide number of fields of human activity and the second half of the eighteenth century in Scotland witnessed a veritable explosion of creativity and industry. Now that the shadow of the '45 had passed, there was something akin to a bursting of the floodgates as the latent energies and talents of Scotland at last found an outlet in positive action.

Although the country as a whole went firmly down the road of recovery, for the Highlanders and the clan system the post-Culloden era was their darkest hour. The bloody persecution of suspected Jacobite sympathisers was pursued with a ferocity which struck out indiscriminately against even those clans which had remained loyal to the British crown. Legislation enacted in 1746 confiscated the estates of the rebels, disarmed the clansmen, destroyed the traditional rule of the clan chiefs and even proscribed the wearing of the kilt or any item of tartan under pain of a seven-year sentence to His Majesty's colonial plantations. This last much resented regulation, known as the Diskilting Act, was repealed in 1782, but it was clearly symbolic of the fact that the real price of defeat at Culloden was the smashing of the clan system itself, and with it of an entire way of life.

How effective was this crushing of the Highland spirit may be gauged from the comments of Dr Johnson who travelled the country in 1773 with James Boswell: 'The clans retain little now of their original character, their ferocity of temper is softened, their military ardour is extinguished, their dignity of independence is depressed, their contempt of government subdued, and their reverence for their chiefs abated. Of what they had before the late conquest of their country there remains only their language and their poverty.' Very soon the Gaelic language was to come under attack on the pretext of the promotion of the Christian gospel, in English of course, by the Society for Propagating Christian Knowledge. Although security was greatly improved, there was still much fear of the Highlands, and those venturing north tended still to take solemn leave of their friends and have prayers said in church for their safe return. The country might be united in theory but the legend of the bandit and cattle-reiver Rob Roy MacGregor lived on, and, as Dr Johnson remarked: 'To the southern inhabitants of Scotland, the state of the mountains and the islands is equally unknown with that of Borneo and Sumatra.'

By contrast, there was substantial progress in the Lowlands. The Improvement was transforming the old chaotic and unproductive tangle of the run-rig strips held under multiple-tenancies into a series of neat, well-drained, enclosed farms which employed the latest advances in agricultural knowledge and machinery. New crops such as clover, potatoes and turnips were introduced, the latter providing much needed winter feed for cattle, thereby preventing the annual slaughtering of livestock at Martinmass. The Age of Reason was quite literally ordering the unruly wilds of the natural landscape which received a liberal sprinkling of neat houses in the Georgian style for the new generation of gentleman-farmers who were taking over from the occupants of the 'fermtouns'. The excess rural population simply drifted off to the growing towns or took ship for the colonies. The spirit of the Improvement was slow in reaching the Highlands but in the

SCOTTISH RENAISSANCE   163

years after Culloden the reorganisation of the estates was pursued with ever increasing vigour. It was the introduction of sheep to the hill pastures which led to the brutal mass evictions of the Highland tenantry towards the end of the eighteenth century. The Clearances were the major factor in emptying the Highlands of their original population, thus fuelling the already rapid flow of emigration to the cities of Glasgow and Edinburgh and to the colonies in America, Australia and the West Indies. By the time of his visit to the Highlands in 1773 the process was, it would seem, already well under way, for Dr Johnson had cause to remark: 'To hinder insurrection by driving away the people, and to govern peaceably by having no subjects, is an expedient that argues no great profundity of politicks.'

On the other hand, agriculture in Scotland was making a profit for the first time, and the money coming from the Improvements provided much of the finance for such ambitious urban developments as the New Town in Edinburgh. Here the crowded tenements of the Old Town, where rich and poor lived huddled together in the greatest intimacy and with the most primitive sanitation, lost their wealthy occupants to the ordered Georgian townscape emerging to the north. Sir Walter Scott, who made the transition from Old to New Town, recalled the atmosphere of the Old Town, the 'democracy of the common stair' and the taverns where lawyers and bankers would receive their clients. By 1822 much of the new urban vision was in place when George IV made his symbolic visit to Edinburgh and declared: 'Good God what a fine sight, I had no conception that there was such a scene in the world, and to find it in my own dominions!' Even today the contrast is powerful; it suffices to compare the elegance of the Georgian House in Charlotte Square with the narrow tenement in the High Street known as Gladstone's Land.

The hopes of those who had campaigned for a capital city worthy of the name had been gloriously realised. From about 1760 to 1830 Edinburgh served as a national forum for a dazzling parade of brains and talents which amounted to a Scottish Renaissance. The city drew philosophers such as David Hume and Adam Smith, poets such as Robert Burns and Sir Walter Scott, artists such as Sir David Wilkie and Sir Henry Raeburn, and the architects Robert Adam and William Playfair. Such names were but the best known of a veritable burgeoning of Scottish creative energy which may be seen almost as a determined effort to redeem the nation's pride in itself, and the new Edinburgh, the 'Athens of the North' was the most palpable symbol of that resolve.

However, even in her hour of glory, Edinburgh was being overtaken by an economically rampant Glasgow. In 1707 Glasgow was a medium-sized burgh of 12,500 people, and, due to the shallow waters of the Clyde, not yet a proper port. The city was much admired by such as Defoe, who wrote: 'In a word 'tis the cleanest and beautifullest and best built city in Britain, London excepted.' This neat and pleasing township was poised for an explosive growth which saw the population increase twentyfold, passing the 250,000 mark at the time of Queen Victoria's accession in 1837. The wealth of Glasgow came initially from the re-export of American tobacco and it was the tobacco lords who put in hand the first phase of the city's development prior to 1776 when the American War of Independence interrupted the trade. Cotton came to the rescue and helped Glasgow to emerge by 1830 as Scotland's boom town with 90 per cent of the country's cotton-spinning capacity. This placed Glasgow's supremacy beyond dispute and laid the foundations for the subsequent industrial phases of iron and steel, ensuring that the nineteenth century belonged to Glasgow just as the eighteenth had belonged to Edinburgh.

Industrialisation was gaining ground even in such remote locations as the Western Highlands where an enormous iron-smelting plant was established at Bonawe as early as 1753. The availability of deciduous woodland for charcoal-burning was the reason for the undertaking; an estimated 10,000 acres of forest were needed to satisfy Bonawe's voracious appetite. This was the largest industrial enterprise in the Highlands,

Floors Castle

employing 600 workers. At Carron near Falkirk sprang up the famous Carron Iron Works which by 1800 was the biggest munitions works in Europe. Steam power, using the revised engine with separate condenser invented by James Watt, unleashed a new generation of machines. In 1828 James Neilson's hot-blast method of smelting iron led to a boom in iron mills in the Coatbridge area close to the coalfields.

Bonawe Iron Furnace

Coal, the fuel of the Industrial Revolution, was mined according to a system more in line with the feudal habits of the Middle Ages than the Age of Enlightenment. Miners were bought and sold along with the pits in which they toiled as so many serfs. Women and children were likewise enslaved in the back-breaking work and lived in conditions which defied description. Indeed, the adverse social effects of the Industrial Revolution were fast becoming evident everywhere, especially in the packed slums of Glasgow which soon became synonymous with urban horror. Even in the service-centre of Edinburgh the Old Town, now abandoned by the well-to-do, became a frightful repository for filth, poverty and disease. More progressive industrialists such as David Dale and Robert Owen attempted to reverse the brutalising trends with their ideas of a new industrial environment at New Lanark; but this was an isolated example and the paternalistic philanthropy of Robert Owen was often resented even by those whom it was intended to help.

The major effect of the industrial era was the rapid urbanisation of the Central Lowlands. Whereas in 1750 only 10 per cent of the population lived in the burghs, many of which were no more than villages, by 1831 20 per cent of the population lived in one or another of the six major towns. The greatest drain of the rural population was felt in the Highlands; despite attempts to set up model villages for manufacture and fisheries such as Inveraray, Campbeltown, Tobermory and Grantown-on-Spey, the trend towards the emptying of the Highlands was unstoppable with the Clearances continuing until about the middle of the nineteenth century, in parts even longer.

Ironically, the reputation of the Highlands was redeemed just as its spirit had been broken and the glens depopulated. The romantic vision of Sir Walter Scott provided a sanitised myth of the Highlands soon after the identity of the clans had been destroyed. The eighteenth-century spirit, which had abhorred the violent anarchy of the natural wilderness, gave way to a nineteenth-century passion for the rugged landscapes and remote Celtic heritage of the north. Tartans, which had been proscribed until 1782, rapidly became the vogue; and there was an outburst of 'tartan mania' especially in the Lowlands and in England. With his historical novels Sir Walter Scott had unwittingly launched the Scottish tourist industry with his romantic presentation of clan folklore and noble vistas.

The new generation of travellers could take advantage of the boom in communications which had marked the second half of the eighteenth century. Although the railways did not reach Scotland until the Victorian age, improvements to the roads had provided plenty of scope for the nation's energies. Thomas Telford, known as 'The Colossus of Roads', had personally supervised the building of 875 miles of long-distance highways in Scotland during his time with the Commission for Highland Roads and Bridges. There are fine Telford bridges at Dunkeld and Craigellachie as well as the Dean Bridge in Edinburgh. John Rennie's magnificent bridge at Kelso, completed in 1803, was to serve as the model for his Waterloo Bridge of 1811 in London. John Loudun MacAdam's skills as a road engineer were eventually adopted in his native country. There was a corresponding improvement in transport. In 1760 there were only two stagecoach services in Scotland, but the number had risen to over one hundred by 1830. This was also the age of the canals, the most dramatic of which was the Caledonian Canal begun in 1803 by Thomas Telford, cutting straight through the Great

Telford's bridge of 1809 over the Tay at Dunkeld

Glen, unconsciously following the route of prehistoric man. There was also a network of narrower canals in the Central Lowlands such as the Forth and Clyde of 1790, the Monkland of 1793 and the Union Canal of 1822 which served for the transport of coal and produce in the rapidly urbanising belt between Edinburgh and Glasgow.

With all the changes that had been wrought, Scotland in 1837 would have been largely unrecognisable to a man who only knew the country as it had been in 1707. The transformation of the land reflected the emergence from the humiliation of the forced merger with England to a dominant economic and self-confident position. The eighteenth century witnessed the passing away of the old order. Noblemen and clan chieftains left their traditional tower-houses for stately residences such as the castles of Inveraray, Floors and Mellerstain, or indeed for a Georgian house in Edinburgh's New Town. The ordered harmony of formal gardens, landscaped parks and enclosed farms created the present appearance of the Lowlands; and the Clearances in the Highlands made for the empty landscapes encountered today. At the same time the industrial heartland of the country with its hundreds of belching chimneys had mushroomed, placing Scotland in the vanguard of contemporary development.

There was, however, a sad note in this grand outpouring of the nation's energies. The Scottish Renaissance, no sooner established, could not be contained within the borders of the country. Already in the mid-eighteenth century the words of Robert Adam had become prophetic for many others: 'Scotland is but a narrow place. I need a greater and more extensive and more honourable scene. I mean an English life.' The brain drain of the eighteenth century, which had included Tobias Smollett, James Boswell and Thomas Carlyle, was to become a general flood in the nineteenth as Scottish talents flowed south and became the lifeblood of the British Empire. The old spirit of Caledonia escaped rather like a genie from the bottle and lived on elsewhere as Scottish farmers, administrators, soldiers and engineers took their skills to the farthest corners of the earth. Nevertheless, Scotland still possessed sufficient human resources to power another 100 years of tremendous expansion in the nineteenth century.

The Taming of the Highlands

Military control of the Highlands had only been attempted intermittently in the course of Scottish history. Even men of the stamp of Julius Agricola and Oliver Cromwell had achieved but a temporary and precarious hold on this wildest of territories where clan feuding and raiding were surpassed only by the fiercest opposition to any outside attempt to impose law and order. Yet in the first half of the eighteenth century the Highlands were to be pacified and the clan spirit broken beyond repair. To this day the Highlands bear the mark of this final unhappy phase in the struggle of the clans against the intrusion of central government.

Already in 1699 the establishment of a number of garrisons in the Highlands had been proposed, but it was not until after the Jacobite rising of 1715 and its abortive sequel of 1719 that effective action was taken. Standard government-style barracks were then built at Bernera, Inversnaid, Kiliwhimin and Ruthven in Badenoch. The latter, now known simply as Ruthven Barracks, are the best preserved of all and still form a prominent landmark to travellers on the A9 near Kingussie. Constructed between 1719 and 1721 on what is probably a thirteenth-century motte the barracks consist of two blocks facing each other across an open courtyard. The two projecting towers at diagonally opposite corners are reminiscent of the Z-plan tower-house. It was the duty of the garrison to police the

Ruthven Barracks near Kingussie

Highlands and disarm the clans. Ruthven Barracks, like others of its type, was in effect little more than a toy fort, for it was not designed to withstand more than a casual assault. Its garrison was obliged to surrender in 1746 to a Jacobite army which had procured field artillery, and it is not without irony that this erstwhile English stronghold served as the rallying point for the defeated survivors of Culloden before the order came to disperse into the hills and glens.

Forts such as Ruthven were part of an extensive military network in the Highlands which was largely the work of the energetic and purposeful General George Wade, who was instructed in 1724 by George I to report on the state of the Highlands and to suggest remedies. As Commander-in-Chief in Scotland Wade also supervised the execution of his proposals. The works carried out or initiated by Wade have proved to be of enduring value, and Wade's name is still associated with over 250 miles of road and over 30 bridges in the Highlands. Many of his roads have been integrated into

today's network but others have survived as magnificent cross-country tracks used only by walkers. Some of the bridges are of note, especially the superb structure over the River Tay at Aberfeldy, a William Adam design of 1733.

Other links in the chain of territorial control in the Highlands were Wade's new strongholds in Inverness and at Fort Augustus; the latter, strategically situated in the middle of the Great Glen, served as headquarters. But as it turned out, the formidable martial aspect of Fort Augustus was mere façade, for it fell to the Highlanders after a two-day siege in 1745 and it was later to be absorbed into a Benedictine abbey which bears the same name. The vulnerability of Fort Augustus, and indeed of the other Hanoverian outposts in the Highlands, during the Jacobite rising of 1745 showed that the English military hold was every bit as tenuous as that of the Romans. The taming of the Highlands was to be more ruthlessly pursued after the defeat of the clans at Culloden the following year.

Wade's bridge over the Tay at Aberfeldy

Prince Charles Edward Stewart

With the wisdom of hindsight the Jacobite rising of 1745 belongs to the annals of famous lost causes and doomed enterprises. It is easy to overlook its achievements, which were not inconsiderable even though short-lived. Although supported by not all of the Highland clans and at best endured by the Lowlands, the '45 was a heroic demonstration of the Scottish spirit of independence, and at least in the initial stages of the revolt it succeeded in shaking the foundations of the Hanoverian military might which had been so painstakingly laid by General George Wade and others. With the exception of Fort William, all the Hanoverian strongholds in the Highlands were taken, and even the military roads were put to better use by the rebels than by the enforcers of law and order.

Although Bonny Prince Charlie commenced his campaign with only a handful of followers and never commanded much more than ten thousand untrained and poorly equipped men, his military successes, notably at Prestonpans, and his triumphant progress through England as far south as Derby, struck terror into the hearts of many; in London there was unfeigned panic and almost an economic crisis with fears of a run on the Bank of England. But the Highlanders found themselves overextended and opted for a retreat back north: a decision which was to lead inexorably to their slaughter at Culloden on 16 April 1746 and the bloody aftermath to the battle as the victorious Duke of Cumberland ravaged the Highlands.

The whole venture lasted just over a year from Charles's landing at Loch nan Uamh near Arisaig on 25 July 1745 until his departure from the same spot on 20 September 1746; and he spent the last five months of his stay in Scotland as a fugitive sleeping rough in the heather or in shepherds' bothies. The trail of his escape is a circuitous route through the Western Highlands and Hebrides which involved many narrow escapes, notably when he donned female costume to disguise himself as the maid of Flora MacDonald, by which ruse he escaped from South Uist 'over the sea to Skye'. Much of the romantic folklore woven about the legend of Bonny Prince Charlie relates to his time on the run after defeat at Culloden; and there is still a lingering pride that no Scot betrayed him in spite of the £30,000 price on his head and the dire punishments meted out to anyone suspected of providing assistance.

Like Mary Queen of Scots, that other hapless child of the Stewart family, Prince Charles Edward has acquired a historical stature beyond his deeds. His fate became inextricably entwined with the melancholy fate of the Highland clans, for the real outcome of defeat at Culloden was not merely the demise of the Jacobite cause but, more importantly, that of the clan system and the final subjugation of the Highlands. The '45 was the last time that the clan chiefs called their children to arms in defence of their independent lifestyle. It is thus fitting that the monument at Glenfinnan, where the standard of the revolt was raised on 19 August 1745, carries a statue not of the Prince but of an anonymous Highlander, one of those according to the dedication who 'fought and bled in that arduous and unfortunate enterprise'.

As for the man himself, the memory of Charles Edward Stewart is but a scattering of personal items such as locks of hair, pieces of clothing, secret portraits and a silver drinking flask, now displayed as sacred relics in a score of castles and museums. His lingering exile in Rome, where he died at the age of sixty-eight, with its episodes of drunken debauchery is all but forgotten. He is remembered as a youthful hero, a romantic figure for whom many a wise man allowed his head to be ruled by a longing in his heart for a Scotland free to pursue its own destiny along traditional lines, a Scotland which had in fact almost disappeared.

The monument to the '45 at Glenfinnan

Fort George

Even before it was constructed, Fort George at Ardersier, on a narrow spit of land jutting out into the Moray Firth, was described by none other than Lt Col. James Wolfe as 'the most considerable fortress and best situated in Great Britain'. It was intended to be so, for the purpose of Fort George was to provide an impregnable base for the Hanoverian armies and thereby efface the humiliating memory of the weakness of Wade's small Highland forts which had proved so ineffective against the clansmen during the '45. There is no more powerful symbol in Scotland of the Hanoverian resolve to crush any resistance in the Highlands than this outstanding fortification which was a model of contemporary practice according to the artillery capability of the time.

The project was conceived in the immediate aftermath of Culloden, and precautions against attack were taken from the very beginning while work was in progress. The 42½-acre site, with enough buildings for a garrison of 1,600 men as well as an artillery unit, amounted in fact to the creation of a small township on a barren strip of land, the largest construction project in the Highlands yet undertaken. During the peak of activity more than a thousand men were employed but numbers fell to less than a hundred as the work approached completion in 1769. This self-contained military settlement possessed, in addition to its barracks, magazine, ordnance and provision stores, a bakehouse, a brewhouse and a chapel. The design by William Skinner, Director of Engineers, was carried out to the highest specification. The brickwork and masonry contract was entrusted to the family firm of William Adam, and much of it was overseen by his sons John and Robert. The cost was correspondingly high and the original estimate of £92,673 19s. 1½d. was more than doubled, coming in at over £200,000 – an enormous chunk of defence spending by the standards of the day.

Curiously, Fort George turned out to be almost obsolete even before its completion. By 1769 there was no longer a military threat to be feared from the Highland clans which had been so brutally and efficiently suppressed. In 1795 the permanent garrison of

Fort George

Fort George was a company of Invalids (that is, men who were no longer fit for active service). Within a single generation the threat of the clans had thus shrunk to a shadow of its former strength. Fort George was never once to be challenged by land or by sea.

With continuing improvement in artillery technology Fort George's impregnability was soon called in question, and in the nineteenth century it was almost abandoned as a garrison and turned over for use as a prison. Against the odds it has survived, miraculously intact, and it still serves partly as the headquarters of the Royal Highland Fusiliers.

Fort George is significant as a splendid example of eighteenth-century military architecture. Its immense ramparts and bastions project like the point of a spear towards the sea. The landward aspect is protected by a huge 'ravelin', a detached triangular work protruding in an aggressive stance. The dramatic symmetrical zigzag of the fortification, still with many guns in place, and the fine preservation of the original garrison buildings provide a scene of outstanding authenticity which is much in demand as a film location. As one surveys the orderly rows of barracks from the wind-swept ramparts it takes little to imagine the empty streets teeming with the bright red uniforms of the soldiers for whom this enormous accommodation was planned, in order that they might ensure the final taming of the Highlands.

Fort George

The Adam Phenomenon

Sir William Bruce had pioneered the neo-classical movement in Scotland with his uncompromising design for the new royal palace of Holyroodhouse, commissioned by Charles II in 1671. Unlike previous architectural innovations patronised by the Stewart monarchy, this time the new courtly style was taken up promptly by the Scottish nobility and in turn even by the lesser gentry. Improved security, combined with growing contacts with England and the Continent after the Treaty of Union of 1707, brought about a revolution in gracious living. The abandonment of the defensive tower-house with its confined vertical arrangement allowed a horizontal conception of the house to emerge. Larger rooms set side by side, taller windows and expansive façades presented all manner of opportunities for a more elegant style of country residence. The old ideas of interior design, notably the painted ceilings which had been favoured for so long, proved unsuitable; the new techniques of working plaster opened the way for a more fanciful approach to decoration.

Sir William Bruce still led the field at the beginning of the eighteenth century, but his reputation as Scotland's premier architect

Hopetoun House, one of the colonnades

was soon overshadowed by a certain William
Adam of Kirkcaldy. Such was the impetus
for architectural progress at the time that
Hopetoun House, first built by Sir William
Bruce between 1699 and 1703, was subjected
to a radical modification and enlargement by
William Adam in 1721, less than twenty
years after completion. Hopetoun House is
particularly revealing about the evolution of
style, for much of Bruce's work has survived,
and the present structure is really a combination of two distinct houses. The heart of
Bruce's neat square house is still intact,
keeping the interiors of three principal
rooms as well as the magnificent wooden
staircase. One might say that a third influence
was also at work, as William Adam's designs
were modified after his death in 1748, when

his sons John and Robert took over the
supervision of the project.

It is quite fascinating to see the combined
efforts of the Adam family enterprise in
action at Hopetoun House. The grandiose
east front intended by William was cleverly
toned down into a simpler but still majestic
version favoured by John and Robert; the
two pavilions linked to the central block by
curved colonnades, designed by one of the
sons – probably Robert – point to the
maturity of the later Adam style. The
shaping of the interiors shows likewise a
gradual assertion of the taste of Robert
Adam. The ideas of William Adam are still in
evidence though there was a perceptible
shift towards a lighter, more delicate look;
and the Red Drawing Room, which was

Hopetoun House, the main block

finished last of all, is without doubt the Adam masterpiece at Hopetoun House. Thus was a noble residence transformed into a stately home of palatial elegance, still something of a novelty in Scotland at the time.

However, not all of William Adam's projects were so lavish in style. In fact, much of the Adam fortune was initially made in the humbler tasks of contracting. As Master Mason to the Board of Ordnance for the

construction of Fort George, William introduced both John and Robert at a tender age to the humdrum realities of project management and client liaison. Although William Adam was generally recognised as Scotland's most demanded architect in the 1730s, his career was by no means plain sailing. Duff House at Banff, designed by William Adam for Lord Braco, was apparently never occupied by its owner who was so angered by the rising costs of the work that he could not

Haddo House

even bring himself to look at his new residence. Duff House has not been well received by architectural pundits who view it as a curious sort of hybrid.

With Haddo House in Aberdeenshire, built between 1731 and 1735 for the 2nd Earl of Aberdeen, William Adam provided a purer rendering of the classical theme which set the pattern for the next generation of country homes. The external appearance of Haddo House was slightly modified in 1880 but the original concept is still discernible;

the entrance was by staircase direct to the first floor or 'piano nobile' in accordance with strict Palladian practice. The interior renovations at Haddo House in 1880 are of particular interest, for they represent an early example of the late nineteenth-century Adam revival in a house designed by William Adam. Architectural fashion had come full circle.

Mellerstain in Berwickshire is a notable joint effort by father and son, for the two wings of the house were built by William in

1725 and were finally connected by the central block between 1770 and 1778 by Robert Adam. Although the exterior follows the style set by his father, Robert's interiors are stunningly his own. The library, dining-room and drawing-room at Mellerstain contain magnificent examples of Robert Adam's mature classical ceilings still in their original colours, designs of exquisite refinement.

Much of Robert Adam's best work is to be found in England, but at Culzean in Ayrshire he produced one of his most original master-pieces, a perfect blend of classical harmony and romantic vision. This imposing house, perched high on the cliffs by the sea, presents an apparently martial façade in the best Scottish tradition but achieves the effect in the most simple and elegant manner with an almost total rejection of ornament, relying instead on the skilful arrangement of the building masses. The only obvious features are the small windows in the shape of a cross and the battlemented parapets. The interior at Culzean appears to be held together by a masterfully conceived oval staircase in the classical manner, a *tour de force* which on its own would secure the reputation of Robert Adam as an undisputed magician at interior design. His work at Culzean also extended to the stable buildings,

Culzean Castle, the staircase

the home farm and a mock ruined arch which marked the main entrance to the house, displaying the diversity of his talents, from palace to farmhouse.

Although Robert Adam made his home in London after his long stay in Italy from 1754 to 1758, he made frequent visits to Scotland where his services were much in demand. Through the Edinburgh office of the family firm he worked on an amazing number of Scottish projects in addition to the country houses with which his name is most often associated. He made a significant contribution to the emerging New Town of Edinburgh where the influence of classical architecture was avidly taken up.

The Adam style, seen in terms of cultural history, represents a triumph of Scottish

Mellerstain House

Culzean Castle

inventive genius on a wider international stage. Robert Adam succeeded in letting his light shine brightly enough to dispel the long shadow cast by English architects of far greater social standing. On the narrower stage of Scotland the Adam phenomenon marked a resounding victory of classical ideas over any lingering mediaeval tradition; but the heritage of the Middle Ages was only in hibernation to re-emerge in the nineteenth century in the guise of the neo-Baronial and the Gothic Revival.

Ann Street, Edinburgh

Athens of the North

During the years 1760 to 1830 Edinburgh underwent a metamorphosis which may be described as a classical butterfly emerging from the chrysalis of the Middle Ages. At last the cramped and insalubrious Old Town found release from its huddled tenements clinging to the Castle Rock, and the people of substance were able to install themselves in a graceful Georgian urban setting of elegant squares, sweeping crescents and broad streets. The contrast between the Old Town and the New could not be stronger; and the remarkable fact about this great and dramatic transformation of the Scottish capital is that it was the direct result of the initiative launched by the citizens themselves. The modestly titled *Proposals for Carrying on Certain Public Works in the City of*

Edinburgh of 1752 argued that economic progress and the quality of life in general suffer untold harm in a run-down urban environment. In the *Proposals*, the renewal of the capital city was advanced as a necessary step to promoting the well-being of the nation as a whole: 'The meanness of Edinburgh has been too long an obstruction to our improvement, and a reproach to Scotland.'

The authors of the *Proposals* provided a valuable description of the inconveniences of the Old Town: '. . . the houses stand more crowded than in any other town in

Charlotte Square, Edinburgh

Europe, and are built to a height that is almost incredible. Hence necessarily follows a great want of free air, light, cleanliness, and every other comfortable accommodation. Hence also many families, sometimes no less than ten or a dozen, are obliged to live overhead of each other in the same building; where, to all the other inconveniences, is added that of a common stair, which is no other in effect than an upright street, constantly dark and dirty.'

More graphic accounts can be found in the

The Georgian House, Edinburgh

writings of such eighteenth-century travellers as Edward Burt, assistant to General George Wade, who succeeded in his desperate attempts to avoid the emptying of the chamber-pots from the upper storeys in the narrow wynds: 'but when I was in bed I was forced to hide my head between the sheets; for the smell of the filth, thrown out by the neighbours on the back side of the house, came pouring into my room to such a degree, I was almost poisoned by the stench.' Ironically known as the 'flowers of Edinburgh' the distinctively pungent aromas of the streets were evidently tolerated by the inhabitants as an unavoidable, albeit unpleasant aspect of city life.

One views the New Town of Edinburgh, as it exists today, as a single entity, as if it were all part of a masterplan; but in reality it emerged in a more haphazard fashion, with various pieces being added at different times and under different circumstances. The key to the whole development was the construction of the North Bridge (1763-72) across the Nor' Loch which opened up a vast area for new housing.

The first part of the New Town, Craig's plan of 1767 of 'the New Streets and Squares

intended for His (George III's) ancient Capital of North Britain', was little more than a straightforward gridiron scheme of three main streets running east-west, with a large square at either end. Yet Craig's plan, for all its simplicity, was a cunning exercise in political allegory, in fact a celebration of the Union of Scotland and England. The two squares were to bear the names of the respective patron saints, St Andrew and St George, and the same idea was repeated in a humbler manner in the naming of Thistle Street and Rose Street. In deference to the Hanoverian monarch the principal thoroughfare was to be George Street. With the exception of St George's Square which was subsequently to be called Charlotte Square, all these names originally suggested by Craig have survived.

The most attractive feature of the First New Town, as designed by Craig, was that it was conceived as a self-contained ensemble with an open outlook in all directions. Initially no architectural guidelines were laid down, and the design of the houses was not a part of the scheme. Those who took up the feus on the land enjoyed considerable freedom of choice in the building of their houses, to the extent that not even the street frontages were of a standard width.

This lack of planning principles led to some fairly mediocre and patchy developments in the early stages. As a counter-measure the Town Council commissioned Robert Adam in 1791 to produce a grand and imposing façade for the frontage of the houses in Charlotte Square. Robert Adam died the following year but the north side of the square was built according to his design and is today one of the highlights of the New Town. It contains the property at Number 7, known simply as the Georgian House, which has been redecorated and furnished in the manner of the day by the National Trust for Scotland.

The concept of a unified design-standard set the pattern for the development of the Second New Town just to the north which was begun in the early years of the nineteenth century; such streets as Heriot Row (1803-8) combine a uniformity of appearance with a great variety of design detail. Ann Street (1817), developed by Raeburn, the portrait painter, presents a charming miniature version of the pedimented centrepiece created by Adam in Charlotte Square. Ann Street, with its unique and delightful front gardens, is the most picturesque address in the New Town. However, the most accomplished piece of unified design on the grand scale is by James Gillespie Graham, whose development of the Earl of Moray's feu between 1824 and 1827 is one of the great achievements of the New Town. This three-part architectural crescendo from Randolph Crescent through Ainslie Place to the magnificent octagonal Moray Place, where the best houses went originally for £5,000, is almost theatrical in effect, but it is a well conceived plan which provides a flawless link between the First and Second New Town.

Hand in hand with these and other residential schemes there sprang up all over the city a number of truly remarkable public buildings as eloquent testimonials to the nascent civic pride of Edinburgh. The first of these was the Royal Exchange (1753-60), adapted from a design by John Adam. The huge Register House does not quite reflect the original design of 1774 by Robert and James Adam but possesses an imposing presence. The interior of St Andrew's Church in George Street is one of the lesser known masterpieces of eighteenth-century Edinburgh. The University began life as a Robert Adam design in 1789 but construction was interrupted for many years during the Napoleonic War; when work resumed in 1815 the completion of the project was entrusted to William Playfair and the magnificent Upper Library was a stunning addition to the Adam plan. In fact, Edinburgh owes more to William Playfair than to any other architect: the Royal Scottish Academy, St Stephen's Church, Surgeon's Hall, National Gallery, Donaldson's School, New Observatory, and New College and Assembly

The Georgian House, Edinburgh

Hall are all the products of his drawing board.

William Playfair was also appointed architect for the ambitious Calton Hill scheme which amounted to the creation of another New Town between Edinburgh and Leith. The rocky outcrop of Calton Hill itself was destined to be transformed into the Acropolis of Edinburgh; indeed some Scots who had seen Athens declared it to be more imposing than the original. The National Monument on the summit of Calton Hill was to be a facsimile of the Parthenon serving both as a memorial to the dead of the Napoleonic War and in a wider sense as a sort of Scottish Valhalla for the great and the good of the nation. This ambitious undertaking ground to a halt in 1829 when the money ran out and only twelve columns had been built. And so it still stands today, 'the pride and poverty of Scotland' as Playfair quipped at the time, a dramatic feature of Edinburgh's skyline. Less conspicuous is the Royal High School (1825-9) by Thomas Hamilton. This, by general acclaim 'the noblest monument of the Scottish Greek Revival', is possibly the building which more than any other makes good Edinburgh's claim to the title of

'Athens of the North'; and Calton Hill, liberally strewn with Hellenistic masonry, has Britain's most bizarre collection of neo-classical architecture.

But with all the wealth pouring into the New Town, the Old Town declined further and rapidly became a dangerously over-crowded slum area for the poor. Those who made the move to the New Town found a more formal, less intimate lifestyle. This was

National Monument, Edinburgh

a small price to pay for the attainment of the goals laid down in the *Proposals*. Edinburgh did become a prestigious forum for national life and provided the stage for that great outburst of talent and ideas which has been so aptly described as the Scottish Renaissance.

Royal High School, Edinburgh

The Landscape of the Improvement

Prior to the Union of 1707 Scottish agriculture had been left very much to its own devices. A chaotic system of smallholdings on short leases, which were parcelled out through intermediaries known as 'tacksmen', had ensured that farming did not amount to more than the most basic form of subsistence. As the Age of Enlightenment called into question many time-hallowed precepts, so too agriculture was subjected to radical scrutiny. Rational minds turned over the problems of increasing productivity, promoting progress and ultimately better profits. In 1723 the Honourable Society of Improvers in the Knowledge of Agriculture was founded, and the entire process of reform became known simply as the Improvement.

The main thrust of the Improvement was to reorganise the very structure of farming by the creation of large, orderly units from the haphazard scattering of 'fermtouns' in the Lowlands and 'clachans' in the Highlands. These tiny communities practised the run-rig system of farming narrow strips of land which were periodically reallocated amongst the members of the group. When a 'fermtoun' or 'clachan' grew beyond a dozen or so houses, a second settlement would probably be established nearby. Methods were primitive and the living precarious with famine always just around the corner. There was rarely any excess for sale, and consequently a paltry economic return on the land.

The enclosures began in the Lowlands in

Sheep grazing at Scott's View by the Eildon Hills

the first half of the eighteenth century and spread to the Highlands after the failure of the Jacobite rising of 1745. There was a tremendous boom in cattle exports to England after 1707; by the 1770s Scotland was sending annually more than 100,000 head of beef in great droves to the markets of the south. These were mainly the small, black native cattle, but in time selective mixing with Lowland strains produced new breeds, such as the long-haired Highland which became such a popular motif in the romantic landscape paintings of the nineteenth century. Profits from trade were invested in agriculture; between 1750 and 1825 there was an increase in farmed land of

about 40 per cent and productivity doubled. New farm buildings, planned villages and efficient estates – physical embodiments of the spirit of the Enlightenment – created the basic pattern of the Scottish farmlands as they exist today.

But the single most dramatic change was brought about by the introduction of sheep-farming on a large scale. It was above all other factors the spread of the sheep walks that was to revolutionise the traditional forms of land use in the Highlands and to bring about one of the most painful social dislocations in the history of the Scottish people, which has come to be known by the deceptively harmless term 'The Clearances'.

Highland Cattle by Loch Awe

The Clearances

In the town of Moffat there is an imposing sculpture perched high in the pose of conquering majesty upon a rocky plinth which dominates the market-place. This great figure is no soldier or empire-builder but a mighty ram, a powerful reminder of the awesome influence of the sheep in Scotland; for it was the spread of this animal which, more than any plague, famine or invasion, was responsible for the permanent emptying of the Highland glens of their

human population in the course of the eighteenth and nineteenth centuries.

The year 1792 in the Highlands was for long remembered as the Year of the Sheep, for the useless protest of the men of Ross against the introduction of the Great Cheviot sheep in their braes marked a turning point; henceforth there was to be only sporadic and always ineffectual opposition to the inexorable advance of the sheep. The heart of the problem stemmed from the fact that the landlords saw fit to drive people from their homes in order to make way for vastly more profitable tenants which yielded rich fleeces and mutton. The Clearances were a widespread phenomenon in the Scottish Highlands ranging from fairly benign resettlements to the notoriously cruel practices on the Sutherland estate, where people were driven from their homes with excessive brutality. The burnings at Strathnaver in particular in 1814 have left to this day a memory of those bitter times. Highland soldiers who had fought in the Napoleonic War returned home to the charred remains of their houses to find that their families had been driven out like superfluous livestock.

Behind the widespread suffering of the Clearances, which filled many an emigrant ship bound for the New World as well as many an overcrowded Glasgow tenement, was an irresistible socio-economic force. With the breaking of the traditional power of the clan chiefs after defeat at Culloden in 1746 a vital link with the ordinary members of their clans was sundered. A chieftain reckoned his power no longer by the number of men he could call to arms but by the amount of revenue he could raise from his lands. Dr Johnson noted in the course of his Highland journey in 1773: 'Their chiefs being now deprived of their jurisdiction, have already lost much of their influence; and as they gradually degenerate from patriarchal rulers to rapacious landlords, they will divest themselves of the little that remains.' But in any case the need for cash was paramount in order to pay for the new luxuries of city life in London and Edinburgh

Statue of the 'Great Sheep' at Moffat

Old Highland home at Auchindrain

being enjoyed by the clan chiefs in their smart new houses.

So thorough was the Improvement of the Highlands that scarcely a trace remains of the old 'clachans'; one of the last surviving examples at Auchindrain near the neat planned village of Inveraray is being kept as a museum of the old type of run-rig communal-tenancy. But the Highlands are more notable for the lack of human settle-ments than for any significant remains. Vast areas which had once filled the ranks of many a regiment were entirely depopulated by the middle of the nineteenth century. When men were desperately needed in 1854 for the Crimean War, hardly a platoon could be mustered in the Highlands; and the recruiters met with the reply: 'Since you have preferred sheep to men, let sheep defend you.'

191

The Heritage of Burns and Scott

The names of Robert Burns and Sir Walter Scott have come to stand as a duo of Scotland's literary glory – yet the two men met on only one occasion, during Burns's visit to Edinburgh in 1786 when Scott was in his teens. Beyond their national stature and their strong sense of Scottishness there are many contrasts between the two men, both in their work and in the circumstances of their lives.

Apart from a brief period when he was lionised by Edinburgh society Burns lived in a series of humble farms and modest lodgings in and around Dumfries and Ayrshire. His birthplace in the village of Alloway he described as an 'auld clay biggin' with rats in the rafters. Now much improved with straw instead of turves on the roof, the house still demonstrates the simplicity of the old style of long dwelling, where the cattle byre is merely an extension of the same structure. In spite of his literary success Burns did not manage to escape the poverty trap, and as a tenant farmer on a number of half-improved holdings most of his energies were exhausted behind the plough. Poor food, strenuous and unremitting labour took their toll of the 'heaven-taught ploughman' until his greatest temporal ambition was a steady job as an exciseman. For Burns life on the farm was the basic reality, and it was the failure of his final venture at Ellisland that broke him in 1791 and caused him to move to a small flat in Stinking Vennel in Dumfries – hardly a worthy address for the man who was already Scotland's most famous poet.

BURNS COTTAGE
Robert Burns the Ayrshire poet
was born in this cottage
on the 25ᵗʰ Jan. A.D. 1759
and died 21ˢᵗ July A.D. 1796 age 37½ years

Abbotsford, home of Sir Walter Scott

All the humble places which are now shrines on the Burns heritage trail, such as Poosie Nansie's tavern in Mauchline and Souter Johnnie's cottage in Kirkoswald or the Bachelor's Club in Tarbolton, are modest stuff indeed set next to the neo-Baronial mansion built at great expense by Sir Walter Scott. This elegantly proportioned country home on the upper reaches of the Tweed is not only the dwelling of a wealthy man but also of a prolific writer and researcher. Abbotsford tells much about Scott. The mediaeval details of the exterior provide the perfect showcase for the collection of historic objects to be found within. The suits of armour, weapons, antiquarian memorabilia

Burns Cottage, Alloway

Ellisland Farm near Dumfries, one of the homes of Burns

such as Rob Roy's sporran and a crucifix once owned by Mary Queen of Scots reflect Scott's passion for Scottish history, so powerfully evoked in his poems and novels. Burns had been moved by the same spirit: 'I have no greater, no dearer aim than to have it in my power, unplagu'd with the routine business, for which Heaven knows I am unfit enough, to make leisurely pilgrimages through Caledonia; to sit on the fields of her battles; to wander on the romantic banks of her rivers; and to muse by the stately tower

or venerable ruins, once the honoured abodes of her heroes.' Sadly, however, Burns concludes that these 'are all Utopian ideas'. Scott, on the other hand, was able to transform the dream into reality. Born into a solid family with a legal background, his not onerous duties as Clerk of the Court of Session gave him ample opportunity to travel the country.

Since his boyhood convalescence at Sandyknowe farm in the Borders Scott had become thoroughly imbued with the romance

Dryburgh Abbey, burial place of Sir Walter Scott

of the past; and Scotland's history, with a generous dose of chivalry and idealism, formed the mainstay of his life's work: the epic poems and above all the series of historical tales known as the Waverley Novels. Paradoxically, the professed revivalist Scott, who published *The Minstrelsy of the Scottish Border*, chose to express himself as a writer in English. Burns, however, whose first publication was *Poems Chiefly in the Scottish Dialect*, stuck largely to the vernacular in his subsequent songs and poetry. Although many of Scott's colourful characters do use the native tongue, Burns speaks it

directly to sing of the sweet and bitter realities of human existence with a raciness derived from his own character and experience. Scott poured out his own feelings indirectly on the broader canvas of Scottish history.

It was Scott's great achievement to heal the gaping wounds of national pride in the post-Culloden era by creating a bridge to the glories of the past and at the same time to help his countrymen accept their present status in union with England. Scott was a historical reconciler and also a consummate public-relations man who masterminded George IV's momentous 1822 visit to Scotland. This huge pageant, with the British monarch in Royal Stewart tartan, was to launch the great Celtic revival of the nineteenth century, a highly successful package of largely bogus Highland folklore, which has been taken up more enthusiastically by the Lowlanders than by the descendants of the Gaelic clans themselves.

Burns, however, was passionately patriotic and opposed to the Treaty of Union:

Fareweel to a' our Scottish fame,
Fareweel our ancient glory; . . .
We're bought and sold for English gold,
Such a parcel of rogues in a nation.

But Burns was not a lover of the Highlands by instinct, although he was emotionally on the side of the clans in the Jacobite risings. He wrote of 'a country where savage streams tumble over savage mountains, thinly overspread with savage flocks which starvingly support as savage inhabitants'. His patriotic soul is clearly revealed in the famous poem 'Scots Wha Hae', which on the surface is Bruce's pre-battle address at Bannockburn but is obviously inspired by more recent struggles. Yet Burns only dabbled in history and his real achievement lay in giving the common man a sense of pride and dignity: the words 'The honest man, though e'er so poor, is king o' men for a' that' is one of his best loved poems in which the words 'A man's a man for a' that' have the stirring quality of a drum-beat.

Scott recalled his memory of Burns over forty years after their original encounter: 'I

would have taken the poet, had I not known who he was, as a very sagacious country farmer of the old Scotch school. His eyes were large and glowed (I say literally glowed) when he spoke with feeling and interest. I never saw such eyes in a human head, though I have seen the most distinguished men in my time.' Yet at the end Burns found himself shunned and penniless. His wild lifestyle, promiscuity and lack of respect for the pretensions of the pious and powerful had gradually isolated him; although, once dead, he was rapidly raised to the great status which he holds to this day.

Scott in his longer lifetime acquired far greater national and European acclaim. In addition to his prolific literary output he found time to promote antiquarian interests, organising trips to historic sites such as Loch Leven Castle, Dunfermline Abbey and St Andrews and founding clubs. He might be called the pioneer of Scottish archaeology. His moment of glory as an antiquarian came in 1817 when he and his colleagues rediscovered the lost Scottish Regalia in an oaken chest in Edinburgh Castle. By the time of his death in 1832 Sir Walter Scott had become a national institution; and the Scott Monument, erected to his memory between 1840 and 1846, still dominates Edinburgh's Princes Street as the largest memorial to a writer in Britain.

Burns too has been honoured by monuments of stone. Most notable is the neoclassical mausoleum over his grave in Dumfries which portrays the ploughman inspired by the muse of poetry, but there is a veritable rash of statues and shrines to the poet in that part of south-west Scotland which has been popularised as 'The Land of Burns', to the delight of the tourist trade.

Through their writings Robert Burns and Sir Walter Scott have acquired a stronger historical presence than even the actual protagonists of the drama of Scottish history such as Wallace, Bruce and Charles Edward Stewart. But the memories of Burns and

Bust of Sir Walter Scott
at Abbotsford

Scott are preserved in contrastingly different manners. The romantic scholar Sir Walter Scott, whose collected works fill a long bookshelf, is revered as a man of distinction both generous and warm to his fellows. Robert Burns, the ploughman-poet and man of the people, whose entire output of songs and poems may be contained in a single volume, representing the final great flowering of the Scots native tradition, arouses feelings of love pure and simple.

The Tenth Rule of the Bachelor's Club in Tarbolton, co-founded by Burns in 1780 stated: 'Every man proper for a member of this Society, must have a frank, honest, open heart; above any thing dirty or mean; and must be a professed lover of one or more of the female sex.' Burns's aim in life was never more than that of the common man: 'In short, the proper person for this Society is a cheerful, honest-hearted lad: who, if he has a friend that is true, and a mistress that is kind, and as much wealth as genteely to make both ends meet – is just as happy as this world can make him.'

Birth of the Industrial Society

At the time of the Treaty of Union in 1707 Scotland was chronically poor and the only form of industry to bring some measure of relief was the spinning and weaving of flax into linen. In towns and villages throughout Scotland in the first half of the eighteenth century the sound of the spinning wheel and handloom were the only signs of economic activity. Although run as a cottage industry the weaving business achieved greater specialisation in some of the burghs such as Dunfermline, Perth, Paisley, Glasgow and Musselburgh, which produced various types of muslins, shawl-cloths, calicoes and damasks. Growth was dramatic, especially in Lanarkshire, and by 1778 there were over 4,000 handlooms in and around Glasgow and in Paisley alone some 1,300 weavers were occupied.

Towards the end of the eighteenth century flax was being ousted by cheaper imports of cotton from the Caribbean and America; the first cotton mills in Scotland were established in 1778 at Penicuik outside Edinburgh and at Rothesay on Bute. In 1807 the first power loom in Scotland went into operation at Catrine in Ayrshire and the mechanisation of the textile industry was to radically transform the booming cottage-industry into the familiar pattern of factory manufacture. The self-employed weaver operating from home was rapidly swept away as the new large mills came rattling into action. It was this economic squeeze on the independent handloom weaver which led men such as William Carnegie of Dunfermline to seek his fortune in America. At Kilbarchan near Paisley handlooms were retained for much longer, and here a peak of production was reached in 1830 when some 800 looms were in use. At Kilbarchan a typical weaver's cottage, built in 1723, has been preserved as an example of the old style of home production with the handloom installed in the semi-basement of the tiny cottage which housed the weaver and his family.

In the early stages of the Industrial Revolution it was the availability of abundant water power which drew the cotton magnates of Lancashire into Scotland. Richard Arkwright helped set up a cotton mill and a new village at Stanley in Perthshire in the 1780s, which by 1795 provided work for 350 people. It was in collaboration with Arkwright that the successful Glasgow cloth merchant David Dale surveyed the upper reaches of the Clyde with a view to starting a much more ambitious industrial project. The site chosen by Dale and Arkwright, and named New Lanark as a symbol of a fresh beginning, had grown by the end of the eighteenth century into a self-contained township of 2,000 inhabitants.

David Dale, although he worked hundreds of poor children from six in the morning until six at night with only an hour's break for food and rest, was still reckoned by the standards of the day as a philanthropic employer; the arrangements he made for housing and education were a marked improvement on the abysmal slum conditions already prevalent in the bursting industrial city of Glasgow. Most of the original mill buildings and housing tenements, originally

Cottage loom at Kilbarchan

Workers' housing at New Lanark

constructed by David Dale, can still be seen at New Lanark, happily unmarred by modern development. The workers were housed in salubrious if restricted accommodation; one family occupied a single room where sleeping space was provided for five to six people by a clever arrangement of hurley beds which were pulled out from beneath the built-in box-beds. Entire streets of these early industrial tenements are still standing in New Lanark in Long Row, Double Row and Rosedale Street. Caithness Row was named in honour of the group of Highlanders who came to settle in New Lanark when their emigrant ship was storm-bound at Greenock. The New Buildings of 1798 form the centrepiece of the community housing, and its elegant classical façade shows how the Adam style was being generally applied at the time; even some of the mills are distinguished

199

by features of classical architecture.

In 1799 David Dale sold New Lanark, lock, stock and barrel, for £60,000 to a group which included his son-in-law Robert Owen, who as managing partner of the enterprise from 1800 to 1825 was to spread the fame of New Lanark throughout the industrialised world. Robert Owen is remembered in New Lanark not for expanding the manufacturing base nor for any novel housing projects but for his pioneering work in environmental psychology. New Lanark for Owen meant above all the chance to put into practice some of his own Utopian ideas for the improvement of society. Central to his beliefs was the conviction that an investment in humanitarian aspects of the lives of the workers would enhance rather than impair profits, and that degenerate characters could be reformed by engineering changes in the environment. In the achievement of these aims he was often hampered by the other partners who did not share the totality of his social vision, but he succeeded nonetheless in two major ventures: the Institute for the Formation of Character and Robert Owen's School for Children.

The Institute for the Formation of Character was built between 1809 and 1816 at a cost of £3,000 which came out of company funds. Through its programme of adult education and edifying recreational activities Owen attempted to reform some of the people who by his own account 'lived in idleness, in poverty, in almost every kind of crime; consequently out of health, and in misery'. In his new school Owen tried to replace the notion of discipline through punishments by a positive approach of kindness. in addition to the basic subjects, the curriculum included singing and dancing. Owen's environmentalist theories were not fully matched by actual results, but New Lanark stands nevertheless as a brave pioneering attempt to reform some of the social ills of industrialised society.

New Lanark is also significant, however, in a strictly material sense as the best preserved and most complete example of an

early industrial mill-town. Its orderly rows of tenements grouped about the huge mills by the raging torrent of the Clyde form the most important site of industrial archaeology

New Lanark, a general view of the industrial settlement

in Scotland. Now no longer a centre of manufacturing the entire township is in the care of the New Lanark Conservation and Civic Trust and is itself the object of contemporary theories of environmental renewal.

GAZETEER 6

Battlefields and Historic Sites
1 Culloden Moor
2 Glenfinnan
3 Loch nan Uamh
4 Prestonpans Battle Cairn
5 Scott's View

Burns Heritage Trail
6 Bachelor's Club, Tarbolton
7 Burns Cottage and Museum, Alloway
8 Burns House and Mausoleum, Dumfries
9 Burns House Museum, Mauchline
10 Ellisland Farm
11 Globe Inn, Dumfries
12 Poosie Nansie's Tavern, Mauchline
13 Souter Johnnie's House, Kirkoswald

Canals
14 Caledonian Canal
15 Forth and Clyde Canal
16 Monkland Canal
17 Union Canal

Castles and Country Houses
18 Abbotsford
19 Bowhill
20 Culzean Castle
21 Dalmeny House
22 Duff House
23 Floors Castle
24 Haddo House
25 Hopetoun House
26 Inveraray Castle
27 Kinross House
28 Mellerstain House

Churches
29 Bowmore Round Church, Islay
30 St Andrew's, Edinburgh
31 St Andrew's, Glasgow
32 St George's, Edinburgh

Communications
33 Telford bridges at Craigellachie
34   and Dunkeld
35 Wade bridges at Aberfeldy and
36   Garvamore

Educational and Cultural Institutions
37 Edinburgh University
38 National Gallery, Edinburgh
39 Royal High School, Edinburgh
40 Royal Scottish Academy, Edinburgh
41 Stirling's Library, Glasgow

Fortifications
42 Bernera Barracks
43 Braemar Castle
44 Corgarff Castle
45 Fort Augustus
46 Fort George
47 Ruthven Barracks
48 Hanoverian fortifications at Dumbarton
49 Edinburgh Castle
50 Stirling Castle

Industrial
51 Bonawe Iron Furnace
52 Museum of Scottish Lead Mining
53 New Lanark
54 Weaver's Cottage, Kilbarchan

Monuments
55 National Monument, Edinburgh
56 Nelson Monument, Edinburgh

Rural
57 Auchindrain Museum
58 Kippen Smiddy

Urban
59 City Chambers, Edinburgh
60 The Georgian House, Edinburgh
61 Hutcheson's Hall, Glasgow
62 Pollok House, Glasgow
63 Register House, Edinburgh
64 Town House, Haddington

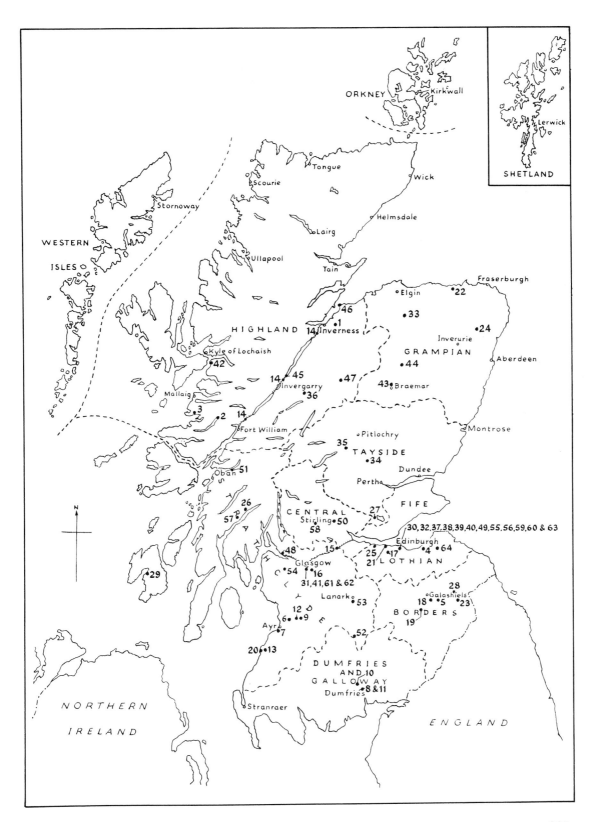

ORKNEY
Kirkwall

SHETLAND
Lerwick

Tongue
Wick
Scourie
Helmsdale
Stornoway
Lairg
WESTERN
ISLES
Ullapool
Tain
Fraserburgh
Elgin •22
46 •33 •24
•1 Inverurie
14 Inverness INVERURIE
HIGHLAND GRAMPIAN
Kyle of Lochaish •44
•42 Aberdeen
14 •45
Invergarry •47
Mallaig •36 43 •Braemar
•3
•2 14
Fort William
Pitlochry
35 •
•TAYSIDE
•34
Dundee
Oban 51 Pertha
FIFE
26 27
57• CENTRAL 30,32,37,38,39,40,49,55,56,59,60 & 63
Stirling•50
N 58 Edinburgh
48 15 •4 •64
Glasgow 25 •17
54• •16 21 LOTHIAN
31,41,61 & 62
29 28
Lanark• Galashiels
53 18• •5 •23
12 BORDERS
6• ••9 19
Ayr •7 52
20•13
DUMFRIES
AND •10
GALLOWAY
Dumfries •8 & 11
Stranraer
NORTHERN
IRELAND ENGLAND

203

7 Victorian and Edwardian Scotland

Sir Walter Scott had written in 1814: 'There is no European nation, which, within the course of half a century or a little more, has undergone so complete a change as the Kingdom of Scotland.' But what Scott had witnessed was about to be overshadowed by the dramatic transformation of the land in the nineteenth century. So great were the changes wrought that the sheer bulk of Victorian Scotland, in terms of building and engineering, is the dominant image of the country today. In this outburst of creative energy Glasgow stands supreme as the flagship of the age, the very expression of the nation's enterprise and growth.

Cotton manufacture had succeeded tobacco re-export as the major source of wealth in Glasgow during the last quarter of the eighteenth century. The introduction of the steam-powered loom early in the nineteenth century allowed cotton mills to be located away from the sources of water power such as the upper reaches of the Clyde, where New Lanark had been established, and right next to the sources of manpower. In Glasgow the industry mushroomed; the number of spinning and weaving factories in the city rose from about 12 in 1807 to almost 50 in 1842. This was just the beginning of an industrialisation process which rapidly turned the urban and neighbouring rural landscape into a panorama of factory chimneys, bleachfields, brickworks and ramshackle tenements. As job opportunities grew, so Glasgow attracted more and more migrant workers from the Highlands and from Ireland as well. The population rocketed from 83,767 in 1801 to 272,324 in 1841, and Gaelic became a significant minority language in the city.

But still the city grew in the second half of the nineteenth century as iron, steel, ship-building and marine engineering added successively to the industrial might of Glasgow, which by 1914 was an extended conurbation and home to more than a million people. This was the high Victorian summer of the city. The Clyde came to dominate Britain's ship-building; by 1870, with the switch from wood to iron hulls, it accounted for 70 per cent of the nation's output, and by 1910 it led the world, providing about a third of international shipping. Glasgow's spirit of enterprise was on a par with London, and the honorary title of 'Second City of the Empire' was carried with pride and confidence. The International Exhibition of Science and Art of 1888 was followed in 1901 by another grandiose International Exhibition, a showcase of the achievements of a century's progress in art, science and industry. The preface to the *People's History of Glasgow* of 1899 conveys the mood of the times:

> The story of Glasgow should be more correctly realised. I should even presume to have it taught in schools and colleges to its future citizens, who might thus learn to honour the spirit which gave Glasgow the ambition to be a hive of useful industry.

The black-house at Arnol, Isle of Lewis

If they knew of the life, the blood, and the treasure spent by the self-reliant and self-respecting generations of the past, and learned the lesson that the city's greatness has been due to corporate endeavour inspired by, and seconding, individual effort, they would be incited to emulate and carry on those activities which have made Glasgow the first municipality in the world and the second city of the British empire.

Glasgow's pride and prosperity found expression in a dazzling array of civic and commercial buildings which are still a prominent feature of the city today. Templeton's Carpet Factory, an Italianate extravaganza, elevated a place of manufacture into a work of art in its own right. The Stock Exchange of 1875 adopted the guise of Venetian Gothic, and Graeco-Roman was the most popular style for a score of palatial banks and insurance companies. The neoclassical works of Alexander 'Greek' Thomson, especially the churches, are most imposing and possess a stylistic vigour which was often missing in the bombastic constructions of the age. The University of Glasgow, by George Gilbert Scott and his son John Oldrid Scott, was much criticised, in spite of its Gothic majesty, as a weak composition overall and has come to be regarded as a missed opportunity to make the best of a magnificent site. But the summation of Glasgow's achievements, as well as the city's high opinion of itself, form the unmistakable message of the City Chambers opened in 1888. This grand gesture of Glasgow at the zenith of its fortunes is no classic beauty, but it makes its point in no uncertain terms; and even in death the Glaswegian meritocrats sought a worthy setting for themselves; the Glasgow Necropolis is a powerful display of monumental funerary architecture.

Out of this tradition of declamatory and eclectic architecture there appeared briefly at the end of the century a revolutionary phenomenon in the person of Charles Rennie Mackintosh. Although the young architect had to cut his teeth on such competition subjects as a Greek public hall, a French Renaissance museum, a classical chapter-house and a gothic railway station, his own views on a style for the future went far beyond the shallow decorative façades favoured by his contemporaries. In a paper delivered to the Glasgow Architectural Association in 1891 on 'Scottish Baronial Architecture' Mackintosh expressed the opinion that style should not be mere imitation of ancient formulae, and that he hoped to 'make the style conform to modern requirements'. In his lifetime Mackintosh, as a pioneer of the modern movement, found acceptance unforthcoming at home. In spite of a handful of commissions which included Queen's Cross Church, Scotland Street School and the Glasgow School of Art, he left Glasgow a broken and disappointed man. He has subsequently attained the recognition he deserves but it is unfortunate that there are not more examples of his work to be found in the city of his birth. Nevertheless, the very existence of Mackintosh in Glasgow as the most avant-garde architect of his day was a sure sign that the commercial success of the city did spawn some rare artistic talent.

Although Glasgow was the supreme example of the Victorian urban achievement, the other main cities in Scotland were also caught up in the rampant development of the age. Even the classical elegance of Edinburgh's New Town, which Ruskin described with horror as 'nothing but square cut stone – square cut stone – a wilderness of square cut stone for ever and ever', was acquiring some prize examples of typical Victorian building, such as the Scott Monument, Fettes College, and the National Museum of

Royal Scottish Museum, Edinburgh

Antiquities as well as some more elegant structures such as the Royal Scottish Museum. In Aberdeen, Dundee and Inverness and in a string of lesser towns there appeared smaller, but not less self-important versions of banks, town halls, schools and insurance offices which provide the familiar nineteenth-century streetscapes of Scotland today.

The proud urban achievements of Victorian Scotland should not, however, disguise the fact that this was also the age of some of the worst horrors of an urbanisation which for a time went out of control. Here again Glasgow provided the most dramatic examples with its notorious slums, overcrowding, disease, pollution and criminality. In the second half of the nineteenth-century life expectancy in Glasgow was as low as 30 compared to a national average in Britain of 46. In 1855 there was a major boost to the city's health with the inauguration of a fresh-water supply piped directly from Loch Katrine in Perthshire. In 1866 the City Improvement Trust diverted some of the energies of the city to the task of slum clearance, and new regulations ensured that the tenements erected towards the end of the century were markedly better than their predecessors. Nevertheless, the brutalising effects of life in Glasgow continued to pose a problem, as can be read from a mass of statistics and accounts published at the time. Writing in 1887 J. B. Russell declared:

Glasgow stands alone with the highest death-rate, the highest number of persons per room, the highest proportion of her population occupying one-apartment houses . . . . It is those small houses which give . . . the striking characteristics of an enormous proportion of deaths in childhood, and of deaths from diseases of the lungs at all ages. Their exhausted air and poor and perverse feeding fill our streets with bandy-legged children.

Old watermill on Skye

The legacy of Glasgow's nineteeth-century housing crisis was to last on well into the twentieth century.

Despite the horrors of urban life for those at the bottom of the heap, people continued to desert the straths and glens of the Highlands in the hope of some form of paid work in the cities. Mostly it was poverty, and even famine, which drove the clansmen from their ancestral lands, but the mass evictions were maintained for much of the nineteenth century and contributed in large degree to the emptying of the Highlands. There are some poignant reminders of the Clearances in the ruins of abandoned settlements but mainly it is the unnatural silence of so many places which speaks of the absence of the native peoples of the Highlands. Those evicted from Glencalvie in 1845 sheltered for a while in the parish church of Croick where they scratched their names on the window panes as a sorrowful souvenir of their fate before the members of the small community went their separate ways, some as far as Australia.

For those that remained in the Highlands the way of life was both spartan and archaic. Numerous examples of the primitive, albeit convivial, black-houses can still be found all over the Western Isles where they continued to be permanently occupied until well into the present century. Some, now modernised, continue to be in use but for the most part they are sad ruins of drystone walls and collapsed roofs of thatch and heather, the last reminders of a native vernacular Scottish architecture. The security of

Interior of an old Highland home at Auchindrain

tenure offered to crofters in 1886 came too late to stem the flow of emigration, but in any case the penetration of the money economy to the remotest corners of the Highlands made life at subsistence level on a tiny croft an unappealing prospect. On a cultural level as well the Highlands were in decline as the Gaelic language, despite the entreaties of Queen Victoria, was fast being eroded by the official promotion of English as the medium for instruction in the schools.

The clan system had already broken down in the eighteenth century but the nineteenth was to witness a significant shift in the pattern of landownership and the management of the great estates. With the growing craze for hunting and shooting, deer-forests came to replace the sheep-walks which had displaced the human communities. Wealthy industrialists from the south purchased huge swathes of the Highlands where they could enjoy the fruits of success in pseudo-feudal manner. Scotland's hills and glens are dotted with the Baronial homes and hunting lodges with the mock castellar effect so popular in Victorian times. The stags' heads mounted on the wall and the game books record the details of the enormous kills. Many of the nineteenth-century generation of Highland landlords have left their mark in spectacular fashion, and none more so that Sir George Bullough of Rhum, whose fantasy Kinloch Castle has a lavish and miraculously preserved interior. Sir George's holiday home on Rhum consumed some £250,000 of his personal fortune at a time when the original budget for the Glasgow School of Art was pegged at £14,000 and the magnificent Templeton's Carpet Factory had been built for only £20,000.

Queen Victoria's love of the Highlands and her frequent stays at Balmoral had done much to promote an aristocratic image of Scotland. It is also claimed that the cult of 'Balmorality' and the pageantry of the Highlands had sparked off the tartan mania of the age. In fact the beginning of the popular interest in the clan and tartan heritage of the Highlands goes back to the founding of the Highland Society in London in 1778 which aimed to keep alive the language and culture of the Gaelic regions of Scotland. In 1822 George IV's visit to Scotland had put the seal of royal approval on the widespread enthusiasm for tartan. By the time Victoria first ventured north of the border in 1842 the Romantic vision of clan folklore and tartan mythology was already in full flight. In 1839 James Logan's *The Scottish Gael; or Celtic Manners as preserved among the Highlanders* had appeared; it contained the first published list of the 'official' clan tartans about which a controversy was raging.

Although voices as eminent as that of Sir Walter Scott had condemned the new clan tartans as bogus – in 1824 he had written: 'I do not believe a word of the nonsense about every clan or name having a regular pattern which was undeviatingly adhered to...' – the demand for ancestral tartans was so strong as to brook any historical inaccuracies. Furthermore, the profits to be made by producing acres of 'correct and authenticated' tartans were irresistible; there were thousands of Scots at home and abroad who grasped at this opportunity to express a deeply felt nostalgia. In 1845 James Logan went into print again with *The Clans of the Scottish Highlands*, a book that was chiefly notable for its superbly romantic illustrations by Robert Ronald McIan portraying noble clansmen in their supposedly ancient dress. These coloured engravings caught the imagination of both Edinburgh and London society and have remained in vogue ever since; framed prints and copies of McIan's drawings are to be found in pubs and hotels all over Scotland. The 1842 publication, entitled *Vestiarium Scoticum*, a bold history of Highland costume by John Sobieski Stolberg Stuart and Charles Edward Stuart, had depicted seventy-five tartans which the authors claimed to be based on documentary evidence from the sixteenth century. But the absence of actual proof did not greatly trouble the tartan enthusiasts of the day. Thus with general connivance there came into being an entire range of tartans which purported to be of the most ancient origin but which were the products of nineteenth-century invention. Likewise the kilt, the sporran and other items of the Highland dress as worn today are modernised and sophisticated versions derived from the simple garb once worn by the clansmen, whose basic item of clothing was the great plaid or 'brechan': one large piece of cloth which was wrapped around both the legs and the body, and served also as a blanket at night.

In addition to the romanticised folklore which still colours the popular perception of Scotland, the Victorian age also brought its technological apparatus to the Highlands in the form of the railways. The second half of the nineteenth century was Scotland's railway age as the steel tracks of the steam trains found their way through the mountains to the wild seaboard of the west. The lines to Oban and Mallaig are of relatively late construction, 1880 and 1901 respectively. The rail network was one of the vital elements in the shaping of the Scottish economy in the Victorian age. With the trains came travellers and tourists for whom hotels were constructed by the railway companies. Soon the Highland fantasy of the castle dwellers could be imitated by a wider public. The advent of the motor car in the Edwardian era enabled improved access to the remotest corners of the land. It is not without irony that, just at the time when modern methods of transport opened up the Highlands to a public imbued with the legends of clan folklore, the clansmen themselves had been effectively cleared from their homes in the heather and were dispersed to the furthermost corners of the globe. In truth, no appreciation of nineteenth-century Scotland is complete without a thought for the absent Scots who sought their fortunes overseas and who made such an essential contribution at all levels to the formation of the British Empire.

Thanks to the invention of photography in the nineteenth century pictorial documentary evidence of Scotland begins with the Victorian era. Thus it is that the sepia prints of travellers in the Highlands and Thomas Annan's sobering views of the slums of Glasgow have become fixed in the memory as our earliest realistic visual record of Scotland. This is perhaps partly the reason why we still tend to perceive Scotland's past through the eyes of our Victorian and Edwardian ancestors. However, the image of the country captured by these pioneers of photography was already as far removed from its ancient roots as it is today. In fact, archaeological research and the conservation of prehistoric and mediaeval sites in the course of the twentieth century have combined to bring the distant past much closer to our world, enabling us to look back beyond the Victorian and Edwardian age with a much sharper focus to the most remote origins of the Scottish heritage.

A Victorian View

Queen Victoria's lifelong passion for the Highlands was so strong and influential that she may be reckoned along with Sir Walter Scott as the main purveyor of a radically new image of Scotland. The wild but poor tracts of the north had generally been scorned by the gentry in the south. Now the Victorian age, already recoiling from the urban and industrial monsters it had begotten, sought refuge in the still savage and untamed aspects of the environment. Scotland's hour had come. Victoria's response to the majestic wilderness of ancient Caledonia was so much in harmony with the romantic yearning of the age that her royal example merely set the seal of approval on the Highland mania already rampant in English society.

She first came under the spell of Scotland in 1842, and the trip north for Victoria and Albert soon became a major event in the royal year. It was in September 1848 that they first stayed at a modest house by the Dee at Balmoral. Victoria noted in her diary: 'All seemed to breathe freedom and peace, and to make one forget the world and its sad turmoils.' Extracts from the account given by Victoria of her travels were published in 1867 under the title: *Leaves from the Journal of our Life in the Highlands*, which confirmed Scotland's noble and aristocratic image and helped in no small measure to promote a tourism industry of lasting value. Indeed, the activities and interests of Victoria and Albert made them perfect prototypes of the travellers of the nineteenth century. Although theirs was a grander production, it was copied in essence by the lesser folk who followed in their wake.

Nature was the main attraction: soaring peaks, rushing torrents, mysterious lochs, purple heather and crimson sunsets. 'Oh! what can equal the beauties of nature! What enjoyment there is in them! Albert enjoys it so much; he is in ecstasies here.' Great expeditions were organised by carriage, on pony and even partly on foot. Many a picnic was held on a windswept summit, and Victoria always noted the vagaries of the Scottish climate: 'Four-hour uphill trek. ... But, alas! nothing whatever to be seen; and it was cold, and wet, and cheerless.' But neither rain nor fog dampened their enthusiasm: 'This solitude, the romance and wild loveliness of everything here, the absence of hotels and beggars, the independent simple people, who all speak Gaelic here, all make beloved Scotland the proudest finest country in the world.'

But love of nature did not prevent Albert from indulging his appetite for blood-sports. In common with most Victorian tourists in Scotland, he was an ardent deer-stalker. Often he would leave Victoria in the royal carriage and disappear into the woods in search of another trophy. Victoria seems to have been totally untroubled by the slaughter, calmly drawing a pencil sketch of a dead stag and reflecting; 'What a delightful day!' Albert even took pot-shots at the gannets as they sailed past Ailsa Craig, but in those days it was quite common to shoot anything with feathers, from eagles to thrushes.

Victoria personified the female tourist ideal with her sketching, water-colours and reading. Landseer's paintings and Sir Walter Scott's writings were her points of reference. In fact *Rob Roy* and *The Lady of the Lake* were always with her 'along with several guide-books, of which we find Black's the best'. In accordance with the romantic Celtic mythology in vogue, Victoria's Highland experience required constant folkloric flourishes. Time and again she noted approvingly that she had been met by reception parties 'in full Highland dress'; of Lord Breadalbane: 'it seemed as if a great chieftain in olden feudal times was receiving his sovereign. It was princely and romantic.' Pipers were usually in attendance to accompany with a pibroch even a simple passage across a loch by rowing-boat and there is a mention of a piper in action during the royal breakfast. Victoria took particular delight in watching the Scottish reels at the

Queen's View at Loch Tummel

annual Gillies' Ball at Balmoral and extended her patronage to the Braemar Gathering. Albert would don full Highland evening dress for dinner, and sport the ludicrously long, hairy sporran which had become an essential part of the 'traditional' Highland costume. Victoria herself would wear a plaid scarf over her shoulder.

Victoria's deep emotional commitment to the Scottish Highlanders caused her to confront the stereotype view of a slothful and dirty people with her own nobler vision: 'There is a great peculiarity about the Highlands and Highlanders; and they are such a chivalrous, fine, active people.' After Albert's death in 1861 her Highland man-

213

servant John Brown from Balmoral became her closest confidant and friend. Her feeling for the people on the estate was that of a mother for her children. She would take pleasure in visiting the old folk in their cottages, offering comfort and gifts to the bereaved. Balmoral gave her the scope for a more caring and personal relationship with ordinary humans than was possible in London where she sat at the official centre of the expanding British Empire.

With the coming of the railway to the Highlands – it reached Ballater in 1867 – Victoria was able to extend the scope of her travels. Everywhere she went there were triumphal arches, reception committees, speeches and nosegays. She would stay at Scotland's finest houses such as Dunrobin, Floors and Inveraray Castle where she was the guest of the wealthy and aristocratic, but she also loved to escape to the simplicity of everyday life, sometimes staying incognito with a small entourage at spartan Highland inns. These escapades did not always turn out for the best, as at Dalwhinnie where all the royal party could muster for supper were 'two miserable starved Highland chickens'. On the trips made by carriage she was at the mercy of horses that refused to pull, luggage that failed to arrive and drivers who took the wrong turning. She even suffered an accident on the Alt-na-Guithasach road when the carriage overturned and ejected her. She did avail herself of the new communications such as the Caledonian Canal: 'a wonderful piece of engineering, but travelling by it is very tedious' (and that, even with a piper at every lock). Like the present royal family, so too Victoria had problems with 'those dreadful reporters' who spied on her and spread scandalous stories of a relationship with her servant John Brown.

Of great historical significance is Victoria's identification with the Stewarts. At Glenfinnan she observed: 'At the head of the loch stands a very ugly monument to Prince Charles Edward, looking like a sort of lighthouse surmounted by his statue ... and here was I, the descendant of the Stewarts and of the very king whom Prince Charles sought to overthrow, sitting and walking about quite privately and peaceably.' Perhaps this sense of being on both sides of Scotland's bloody conflict allowed her to play the role of royal reconciler, for Victoria certainly reinforced Scotland's pride in itself and helped the people to come to terms with the past: 'this beautiful country, which I am proud to call my own, where there was such devoted loyalty to the family of my ancestors – for Stewart blood is in my veins, and I am now their representative, and the people are as devoted and loyal to me as they were to that unhappy race'. Passing through Glencoe, the scene of the horrible, government-instigated massacre of the MacDonalds in 1692, Victoria simply but earnestly writes: 'Let me hope that William III knew nothing of it.'

Under Victoria's rule Scotland received by way of compensation for its loss of sovereignty a long and unswerving support from the Queen-Empress, and Balmoral became at times a centre of imperial diplomacy with visits from Empress Eugénie and Tsar Nicholas II. So strong still is Victoria's aura that her presence appears to hang over the hills and lochs. It is as if the nineteenth-century painters such as Landseer have provided the definitive artistic evocation of the Scottish Highlands which still best expresses our feelings about the wild and romantic landscape which so attracted Victoria and her contemporaries. Victorian Scotland lives on also in the countless monuments erected in honour of the monarch, and most potently in the great castle at Balmoral built by Victoria and Albert between 1853 and 1855 where they spent their happiest hours.

Dunrobin Castle

Common Life in the Highlands

With her ecstatic vision of Highland solitude it is not surprising that Queen Victoria did not miss the thousands of Highlanders who had once inhabited the remote glens, and who had either emigrated or been evicted by force in pursuance of the Clearances. It is interesting to note that during a visit to Dunrobin, the princely castle of the Duke of Sutherland, Victoria wrote in her diary of 'my dear Duchess of Sutherland, who was adored in Sutherland'. This view appears to be at variance with the response given to the Duke of Sutherland in 1854 by an elderly tenant, who explained why no soldiers could be mustered on the Sutherland domain: 'I am sorry for the response your Grace's proposals are meeting here, but there is cause for it and a genuine cause . . . These lands are now devoted to rear dumb animals which your parents considered of far more value than men. I do assure your Grace that it is the prevailing opinion of this county, that should the Czar of Russia take possession of Dunrobin Castle . . . we could not expect worse treatment at his hands than we have experienced in the hands of your family for the last fifty years . . .'

It was quite natural that Victoria should have acquired most of her information about the basic conditions in the Highlands from her rich and noble hosts and that she automatically shared their attitudes. However, she did show some interest in the way of life of the common folk and even noted in her diary details of such developments as the disappearance of the old 'run-rig' farming communities. During a visit to Inveraray she copied an account given her by the Duke of Argyll and faithfully repeated the correct opinion on 'run-rig': 'This very rude system is quite incompatible with any improved culture, but it is an extremely ancient one.' Of the settlements at Achnagoul and Auchindrain we learn from Victoria: 'They are said to be the only two villages of their kind in existence in the Highlands.' But in the main such precise sociological information is rare and Victoria's eye was generally drawn to the noble summits and the folkloric touches.

Nevertheless, she could not help but notice the poverty of many Highland villages: 'The cottages along the roadside here and there hardly deserve the name, and are indeed mere hovels – so low, so small, so dark with thatch, and overgrown with moss and heather, that if you did not see smoke issuing from them, and some very ragged dirty old people, and very scantily clothed, dishevelled children, you could not believe they were meant for human habitations.' But in the same breath, as if recoiling from the reality of destitution, Victoria continues gaily: 'They are very picturesque and embedded in trees, with the heathery and grassy hills rising above them.' At times one can almost sense a shudder of distaste at what she sees: 'Tomintoul is the most tumble-down, poor-looking place I ever saw – a long street with three inns, miserable dirty-looking houses and people, and a sad look of wretchedness about it.'

Victoria did not visit the Outer Hebrides but did undertake a cruise of 'the western Lochs and Isles' which she found to be 'so beautiful – and so full of poetry and romance, traditions and historical associations'. Yet she did note as she sailed past Coll and Tiree: 'The inhabitants of these islands have, unhappily, been terrible sufferers during the last winter from famine.' On the banks of Loch Lomond she observed 'some very pretty villas' and more significantly: 'So many of the finest, largest estates in the Highlands have passed into English hands . . .', a process which her royal patronage helped to accelerate as wealthy industrialists from the south followed in her footsteps.

Thus through the pages of Victoria's *Leaves from the Journal of our Life in the Highlands* we obtain fleeting glimpses of

Remains of past occupation in the Western Highlands

some of the underlying processes which were reshaping the face of the land and the life of the people. Poverty and famine were contributory causes to the emptying of the Highlands along with the Clearances themselves. Victoria even described the new concept of crofting in the nineteenth century, 'where such crofters or very small cultivators as remain are generally separate from each other – each living on his own croft'. In fact, the very idea of the smallholdings was to provide such a low level of subsistence that the crofters would be obliged to work for their living in the fisheries or kelp manufacture on the coast. The crofters were generally opposed to any form of organised labour imposed on them by others and campaigned to obtain larger crofts and greater security of tenure. The Crofters' Commission established by an Act of 1886 did go some way to meeting their demands but the croft remained in essence only a marginal farming unit.

The legislation came too late, however, to help many crofters and only some 15,000 remain in the whole of Scotland, mostly in the Hebrides. Examples of their traditional black-houses can still be seen, especially on Skye and Lewis of the larger islands, and several have been conserved as museums to illustrate a simple way of life which disappeared only in the course of the present century.

The typical black-house, as at Arnol on Lewis, was a long structure of loose stones formed to make a double wall. The cavity was filled with peat-mould and earth for insulation. The roof timbers rested on the inner wall so that a wall ledge remained exposed. This was covered by turves and thus provided some choice grazing for the sheep. The roof itself was of heather, turf or straw. Sometimes there was not even a smoke-hole, for according to the old tradition the soot deposited in the thatch by the peat made excellent fertiliser.

The black-house had one common entrance for both the cattle byre and the living quarters so that the beasts and humans dwelt in the greatest intimacy under the

same roof. Usually there were no windows; the only source of natural light was through openings in the roof. Careful attention was given to drains, and as the nineteenth century progressed so small improvements were introduced, such as wooden partitions and stone paving slabs on the floors of beaten earth. Family life centred around the cook-pot hung over the peat fire, and a snug conviviality made up for any lack of comfort or convenience.

The remaining crofters, now in much improved houses, are all that remains of the lower orders of clan society who once inhabited the Highlands. The combination of social and economic forces working against

The black-house at Arnol, Isle of Lewis

the old ways proved too strong. By the end of the nineteenth century sheep had replaced men as the main occupants of the Highlands. However much one is shocked by the brutality of the Clearances, it is difficult to imagine how the land could have supported such large numbers in anything other than abject poverty. Yet the forced emptying of the Highlands clearly went too far. By a twist of irony the sheep were themselves to be cleared on some estates to make way for deer, an even more lucrative prospect given the vogue for hunting among the rich.

By the time of Victoria's death in 1901 the Highlands consisted of large estates, many with deer-forests and Baronial mansions in nostalgic emulation of the Middle Ages. Where once small communities had been scattered about, only the occasional sportsman in tweed would be seen, and only the half-buried ruins of the old 'clachans' in the heather bore witness to the host of clansmen who once eked out a living in the rugged splendour of the glens.

Temples of Commerce

Glasgow's economic boom spanned the length of the nineteenth century, not running out of steam until the end of the Great War in 1918. It must have seemed to many Glaswegians at the time that they were on an eternally ascendant curve of prosperity, and this sense of pride and self-confidence found expression in a heritage of commercial architecture overshadowed only by London. But in a sense Victorian Glasgow is more impressive than the British capital on account of the sheer concentration of its buildings. Glasgow's rich collection embraces styles ranging from Greek Revival, Venetian and Gothic to Art Nouveau together with many hybrids which escape any particular label.

Three examples serve to illustrate the diversity of the phenomenon.

Gardner's at 36 Jamaica Street is a masterpiece of the glass-and-iron type of structure which is happily in an excellent state of preservation. Even the original lettering on the horizontal beam between the first and second floors has survived. The exceptional lightness of the building is achieved by subtle variations in the size and shape of the windows. The art of the design lies in its simplicity for it does not attempt to disguise its iron frame but makes a virtue of it. Designed by John Baird in 1855 Gardner's belongs firmly to the period in the 1850s when glass-and-iron construction was at its peak in Glasgow. Several other examples of the type have survived in the city but Gardner's is the most accomplished and graceful of all.

Quite the most surprising commercial

Templeton's Carpet Factory, Glasgow

building in Glasgow is Templeton's Carpet Factory of 1888-90. The firm 'as patrons of the arts, resolved not alone in the interests of the workers, but also of the citizens, to erect instead of the ordinary and common factory something of permanent architectural interest and beauty'. In this they certainly succeeded. The red terracotta and glazed polychromatic brickwork with a golden frieze reminiscent of a carpet design may be viewed as a gigantic advertisement for the firm's wares. Yet it is more than a publicity

Gardner's Warehouse, Glasgow

221

The 'Hatrack' in St Vincent Street, Glasgow

stunt. With its bright colours, Venetian Gothic windows and Guelfic battlements it is a fanciful imitation of the Doge's Palace and one of the internationally famous examples of ornamental brickwork. Yet for all its exotic extravagance Templeton's Carpet Factory is completely functional within.

The tiny office building by James Salmon junior at 144 St Vincent Street is known as the 'Hatrack' on account of its narrow 29-foot frontage. The remarkable design of 1899 stems directly from the need to bring light

into the building. The façade is conceived as a brilliant composition of interlocking bay windows and the stonework is almost reduced to nothing. Not one of the ten storeys resembles any other and there is a delight in style and decoration which brings the Hatrack firmly into the realm of Art Nouveau. The influence of Mackintosh is most apparent in the charming barrel-shaped balconies as well as in such internal features as the lift hall. This is a small jewel in a city which is more famous for its monumental works of architecture.

Town House, Aberdeen

Municipal Splendour

New and worthier accommodation for the administration of Scotland's cities went hand in hand with their growing prosperity. Scottish Baronial, with its castellated façades adorned with round corner turrets and conical roofs, was one of the most popular styles of the municipal architecture of the nineteenth century. It attempted to stress an imagined Scottish tradition. One of the finest examples of the type was built by the city fathers of Aberdeen. Their Town House of 1868, designed by Peddie and Kinnear,

Exterior of Glasgow City Chambers

was directly inspired by the fashionable nostalgia which has its roots in the romantic movement unleashed by Sir Walter Scott at the beginning of the century.

When it came to Glasgow to commission a new municipal building to grace George Square the aim was to produce something on a more extravagant scale. The public competition drew entries which on their own would provide material for a catalogue of Victorian architecture. The winning design by the London Scot William Young is a grandiose conception. Glaswegians had been badly shaken by a major financial crisis in 1878, and the new City Chambers project must have been perceived as an opportunity to restore the confidence of the business community. Work began in 1883 and was completed in 1888. It was thus a late gesture of civic pride and may be regarded as the summation of Glasgow's amazing achieve-

ments in the course of the nineteenth century.

The building is dominated by a great tower with a wealth of Renaissance detail, and the main front displays a stunning array of styles – French, Flemish and Venetian. There is a riot of sculptural decoration, a feature which has drawn the criticism that 'the sense of wealth in the place is too insistent'. Yet, as if the exterior were not lavish enough, the interior emphasises the point even more. The loggia, grand staircases and reception rooms as well as the Council Hall itself are a powerful expression of Victorian opulence. Italian marble, Spanish mahogany, stained glass, faience, alabaster, gilt friezes, mural paintings and caryatids combine to overwhelm the onlooker.

This majestic status symbol of the 'Second City of the Empire' was appropriately inaugurated by Queen Victoria in 1888. Over

The staircase of Glasgow City Chambers

the years industrial grime had almost completely obscured its beauty but City Chambers has recently been cleaned to reveal the full glory of its façade of Polonaise and Dunmore stone. However, for all its Victorian magnificence, Glasgow's City Chambers is not a genuine stone building but merely a stone front on a structure of common brick. Like so many of the great rhetorical gestures of the age it contains an element of sham; but it works and this last grand flourish of municipal splendour is a worthy tenant of the east side of George Square.

Seats of Learning

New university buildings were another major achievement of Victorian Scotland, and those constructed at Gilmorehill in Glasgow in the 1870s are the most notable of their generation. Glasgow University had been founded as early as 1451 and had been rehoused in a fine range of seventeenth-century buildings. The site of the Old College in the High Street found itself in the thick of Glasgow's industrial and urban boom in the first half of the nineteenth century, and the problems of noise and pollution as well as the need for expanding teaching facilities made it desirable to move to a more salubrious location.

This was made possible in 1863 when the City of Glasgow Union Railway Company purchased the site of the Old College for use as a goods yard and the £100,000 from the sale provided the funds for the beginning of the new University of Glasgow at Gilmorehill. George Gilbert Scott, the architect of London's St Pancras Station and government offices in Whitehall, was entrusted with the commission. Despite his name, Scott was a London architect, and there was some opposition to him as well as to his Gothic Revival

The undercroft of Glasgow University

design, which was not well received by the neoclassical lobby, which included Alexander 'Greek' Thomson.

Nevertheless, George Gilbert Scott's design for the University of Glasgow was carried out and the first buildings were occupied in 1870. Funds ran out and work had to be suspended until 1877 when gifts from the Marquis of Bute and a local shipbuilder, Charles Randolph, provided the finance for the Great Hall of 1882. The design of this magnificent structure was by John Oldrid Scott, son of the original architect, and it is still the heart of the University with its 'soaring mediaeval romanticism' resting on a vaulted undercroft of great technical accomplishment. John Oldrid Scott was also responsible for the spire of open-work stone which is such a dominant feature of the Glasgow skyline. Although new buildings have been added at intervals to meet the varying needs of the times, the essence of Glasgow University is still contained in the work of George Gilbert Scott and his son John Oldrid, which forms one of the most prominent displays of Victorian architecture in the city.

Glasgow University

Gardens and Glasshouses

John Knox had spread the notion that ornamental gardens were a frivolity but this proved to be no less ineffective an obstacle to the art of gardening in Scotland than the northerly latitude of the country. In fact one of the most enchanting gardens in Scotland, Inverewe in Wester Ross, lies as far north as Cape Farewell in Greenland. Yet thanks to the warming influence of the Gulf Stream the locality enjoys such a benign microclimate that it can sustain some species of flora from regions as diverse as Central America and the South Pacific. The Gulf Stream was, however, the only positive attribute of the windswept peninsula known in Gaelic as Am Ploc Ard (the high lump). It was not on the face of it a promising spot for a garden; but in 1865 Osgood Mackenzie, third son of the Laird of Gairloch, set about with true Victorian zeal to transform the twenty-four acres of red Torridonian sandstone, totally barren but for the heather and a dwarf willow clinging on in the shallow peat, into an exotic woodland which now contains some 2,500 species of plants.

An exotic bloom at Inverewe

Before his death in 1922 Osgood Mackenzie saw the realisation of his dream. He began by planting a wind-break of Corsican and Scots pines so that by 1880 it was possible to introduce eucalyptus and several species of rhododendron. Adding plants and trees from such exotic lands as Tibet, Sri Lanka, Brazil, China and Japan, he created a unique natural environment, which was described by an eminent horticulturist as being in part like some 'wild corner in Burma or Northern China'. Inverewe is a classic tale of Victorian achievement, an individual effort funded by private means. Even the soil had to be transported in creels before the trees and shrubs could be planted. Just how daring was the endeavour in this inhospitable region was shown in 1983 and 1984 when winds in excess of 120 m.p.h. uprooted more than 150 trees. The wonder of Inverewe is that it should exist at all.

In the nineteenth century the craze for importing exotic plants and flowers was widespread in Scotland as in England and led to the expansion of botanic gardens in Edinburgh, Glasgow and other cities of importance. Along with the flora came some remarkable examples of glasshouse architecture to accommodate them, notably the 1858 Palm House in Edinburgh and the magnificent Kibble Palace in Glasgow's Botanic Gardens. Originally built at Coulport on Loch Long in 1860 it was re-erected on its present site in 1873 and provided with a cruciform entrance hall. The main feature of the Kibble Palace is the central rotunda, 471 feet in circumference, a light and elegant structure resting on thirty-six iron columns. It was once used as a concert hall and for meetings but it now contains a riot of tropical vegetation which provides a dramatic background for a stunning display of Victorian white marble statues.

Kibble Palace, Glasgow

Memorials to the Dead

Doubtless the untimely death of the Prince Consort in 1861 had something to do with Victoria's seemingly obsessive taste for bizarre and extravagant funerary architecture, but in this she was very much in tune with the fashion of the age. For throughout Britain the nineteenth century has left its mark with the relics of an unparalleled production of memorials to the dead. The eighteenth-century custom of filling graveyards with tombstones which almost obscured the church was taken a stage further by the Victorians. Their tombs and mausolea were of such ambitious scale that specially laid-out cemeteries became necessary. In keeping with its wealth and pre-eminence among Scotland's cities it was only natural that Glasgow should build the most impressive of these 'cities of the dead' in order to house its illustrious deceased in a style befitting their status and achievements.

The Glasgow Necropolis – perched on a hill behind the Cathedral and the Royal Infirmary – is a testimonial to the merchants and industrialists of the city. Just as these energetic and resourceful men had developed new residential suburbs away from the noise and filth of the centre, so they sought in death a location more salubrious than the old burial grounds which were already over-flowing with the victims of disease and epidemics. Significantly, the Necropolis was not patronised by the aristocrats but almost exclusively by men of humbler origins who rose through their own endeavours to fame and fortune. It was thus yet another mani-festation of Victorian Glasgow's commit-ment to the ideal of self-improvement and material advancement.

The site of the Necropolis, owned by the Merchants' House, previously served as a park with a magnificent city panorama. A soaring monument to John Knox crowned the summit of the hill. In 1831 John Strang, Chamberlain at the Merchants' House, put forward a proposal to emulate the famous Parisian cemetery Père la Chaise by con-verting the park into 'a much wanted accom-modation for the higher classes' which would be 'respectful to the dead, safe and sanitary to the living, dedicated to the Genius of Memory and to extend religious and moral feeling'. There followed a compe-tition in 1831 for plans to create an ornamental cemetery and the work was duly carried out. The first interment took place in 1832, since when there have been more than 50,000, and 3,500 tombs have been built. All plans and inscriptions were scrutinised in order to exclude any of 'very bad taste', for the business of a worthy interment was taken very seriously indeed. In the course of time there were extensions to the Necropolis, but the choice positions were close to the column of the John Knox monument where the hill literally bristles with stone memorials.

The Glasgow Necropolis became so popular with the living as well that it became one of the city's major tourist attractions. In the course of just one month, July 1878, 13,733 people were counted visiting the cemetery. As early as 1836 Laurence Hill published his pamphlet *A Companion to the Necropolis*, and in 1857 this was followed by George Blair's *Biographic and Descriptive Sketches of the Glasgow Necropolis* which put beyond any doubt this 'dreamlike vision of Attic splendour'. During a visit to the Cathedral in 1849 none other than the Prince Consort had 'expressed himself delighted' with the view of the Necropolis.

Sadly, the Glasgow Necropolis is no longer the prestigious place it once was. The depredations of time and vandalism have taken their toll. But it has retained all the interest of its bizarre collection of exotic funerary architecture which rivals the ex-travagant buildings of Victorian Glasgow arrayed in the city below. All of the fashion-able styles of the age are in evidence, from the Greek and Egyptian to the Gothic and neo-Norman as well as some curious hybrids. The William Rae Wilson monument is an octagonal domed sepulchre in the Arab style, and the Egyptian Vaults, built in 1837 for the temporary housing of corpses, is outlandishly impressive. As with many a Victorian creation the moral lesson was not hard to find. George Blair, in his 1857 guide, posed the question: 'Who is not made better and wiser by occasional intercourse with the tomb?'

Such was the Victorian passion for memorials to the dead that they were liberally

Scott Monument, Edinburgh

displayed in the streets and public squares as well as in the cemeteries. Of those commemorated none achieved greater eminence than Sir Walter Scott. Not only does he occupy pride of place atop a column in Glasgow's George Square, but his monument on Edinburgh's Princes Street is a major landmark of the Scottish capital. It took six years to build, and although it is regarded by some as an alien Gothic monstrosity it is now inseparable from the popular image of Edinburgh.

The Tenement House, 145 Buccleuch Street, Glasgow

The Tenement

It is well known that Glasgow is the city of tenements but the word has unjustly acquired a pejorative connotation. Its original derivation was from the Latin, meaning a holding or plot of land, from which the word 'tenement' in Scotland came to denote a particular form of urban housing erected on narrow plots in the city centre where land was at a premium. The tenement evolved as a multi-storey dwelling which contained separate apartments on each floor, and entrance for all was by a common stair. As

with other forms of urban architecture there were different types of tenement which reflected the various stages of its architectural development.

Glasgow's present stock of tenement housing has its roots in the first half of the nineteenth century, when huge numbers of poor people crammed themselves into the old dwellings of the city centre close to the cotton mills. In order to cater for this flood of humanity private landlords constructed rows of tenements. This first generation of industrial housing was predominantly of brick, three storeys high, and packed closely together to the virtual exclusion of air and light. The overcrowding and lack of hygiene

led to some fearful outbreaks of cholera; the epidemics of 1848-9 and of 1853-4 caused the death of 3,772 and 3,885 persons respectively. As a result of growing social conscience it was decided to take action, and the City Improvement Trust was established in 1866 in order to tackle the problem of the slums by enforcing minimum standards of space and hygiene as well as limiting the number of occupants in each tenement.

Consequently, the second half of the nineteenth century saw the arrival of a new generation of improved tenements which are still the hallmark of Glasgow's inner city domestic architecture. During the peak years of 1872 to 1876 some 21,052 tenement houses were authorised in such districts as Dalmarnock, Govanhill, Springburn and Maryhill. At the same time the middle classes were seeking a more rural lifestyle in the suburbs, but there was also a tremendous boom in tenements of a superior type for professional people in districts such as Garnethill and Sandyford.

Unlike the great public buildings the rows of tenements – with some exceptions – were not designed by famous architects but by anonymous builders with no great stylistic ambitions. Nevertheless, a generic style did develop, with motifs borrowed from the Renaissance *palazzi* of Italy. Great attention was given to the arrangement and decoration of the standard format windows in order to relieve the monotony of the longer rows of tenements which stretch away as far as the eye can see. Tenement building virtually

Sitting-room of the Tenement House, Glasgow

came to a halt at the beginning of the twentieth century and the needless demolition of many in order to make way for some disastrous high-rise schemes has seriously depleted Glasgow's stock of tenement housing.

In recent years there has occurred a new awareness of the quality of the traditional form of tenement and many rows have been cleaned and modernised to provide fine contemporary urban homes. One tenement in the Garnethill district of 1892 vintage has even been acquired by the National Trust for Scotland as an example of the type. The three-room flat at 145 Buccleuch Street, now known simply as the Tenement House, is a miraculously preserved specimen of domestic arrangements in Glasgow in the early years of the twentieth century. It was kept almost as a living museum by the tenant Miss Toward from 1911 to 1965 and is an intimate record of life in a superior Glasgow tenement – a far cry from the slum dwellings usually associated with the word.

The kitchen of the Tenement House, Glasgow

Edwardian Fantasy

On the tiny island of Rhum is a building which has been described as akin to 'a vision of St Pancras Station in the middle of the Sinai desert'; but Kinloch Castle is in fact only a more spectacular version of a type of retreat in the Highlands and Islands which was extremely popular with the sporting gentlefolk of Victorian and Edwardian days. It speaks of an age when Scotland came to be regarded by those with wealth as consisting of little more than an expanse of private sporting estates. Vast tracts of the Highlands, some as big as the minor English counties, changed owners repeatedly in the course of the nineteenth century; and many of these men of substance chose their Scottish domains as the context in which to act out their whims and fantasies. The Baronial dream was the most common, and there is no finer illustration of the trend – nor so well preserved – than Kinloch Castle.

The Isle of Rhum changed hands three times in the course of the nineteenth century.

Kinloch Castle, Isle of Rhum

A Mr Campbell acquired it from the 2nd Lord Salisbury, father of the Victorian Prime Minister, and in turn sold it to a Mr John Bullough, a successful Lancashire industrialist. It was his son George who inherited in 1891 the phenomenal wealth of the Bullough estate, which included the Isle of Rhum. George, with his unfeigned love of the gentlemanly pursuits of rod and gun as well as cruises in his private yacht, took to his inheritance of a Hebridean island with an enthusiasm whose physical expression on Rhum can still be admired.

George Bullough commissioned his new castle from the London firm of architects Messrs Leeming and Leeming. No expense was to be spared. The red Arran sandstone was brought in by boat, as were the craftsmen who came mainly from Lancashire. It is part of the Bullough legend that the workmen were paid a daily supplement for wearing a kilt, a further indulgence of the owner's taste for Highland fantasy. The style chosen for the building, not surprisingly, was Baronial. But in spite of its obvious artificiality the design has been charmingly thought out. The picturesque towers and battlements and the covered colonnade which surrounds the house perfectly express the leisurely character of the building's function.

The interior is a lavish display of Edwardian clutter. The furnishing of the castle is anything but Scottish: most items came from fashionable stores in London's Tottenham Court Road and many bits of oriental bric-a-brac were collected in the course of a world tour on the Bullough yacht. A full-length portrait of Sir George dressed in a kilt presides over the forest of stags' antlers which adorn the hall. The house is literally stuffed with personal mementoes, such as Sir George's photo albums in the study and riding boots in the bedroom, and Lady Monica's music scores bound in red leather lying on the piano as if she had just stepped out into the garden and would return at any moment to resume her playing. Under the stairs there is a huge music machine known as the 'orchestrion' which can play the

Main hall of Kinloch Castle, Isle of Rhum

favourite tunes of the Bulloughs, such as 'Ma Blushin Rosie', from large rolls of perforated card.

The air of suspended animation about Kinloch Castle is due to the terms of the sale of Rhum to the Nature Conservancy Council in 1957 which stipulated that the house and its contents should be kept in their original state. Thus has been preserved what John Betjeman described as 'an undisputed example of pre-1914 opulence' and 'the fine embodiment of good King Edward's reign'. But Kinloch Castle also stands for the taking over of much of the Highlands by the new financial aristocrats, the barons of the industrial age.

A Style for the Future

Sir George Bullough's Edwardian fantasy of Kinloch Castle was barely finished when in 1902 the young Glasgow architect, Charles Rennie Mackintosh designed a house in Helensburgh which obviously belongs to a different age, indeed almost to a different world. Instead of the brash parade of self-conscious Baronial features so much in vogue at the time, Mackintosh's Hill House presents a slightly self-effacing, thoroughly watchful external aspect. Here is a totally different reference back to the native tradition, in this case to the simple values of the vernacular style with its insistence on security and protection in a harsh environment. The use of the old technique of harling hides the joints of the building and gives it a curious modelled effect as one element flows into the next. Small windows and a circular turret with a conical roof are unmistakable reminders of Scotland's pre-Adam building style.

But the real surprise at Hill House comes within. Instead of the clutter of conflicting furniture and heavy decoration of Victorian and Edwardian interiors, all is order, space, harmony and beautiful simplicity. For a Scotsman there is hardly one recognisable form, although a Japanese would find familiar elements in the elegant lines of the lamps, tables and chairs. Attention has been given to every last detail: furniture, carpets and curtains have been designed to create a harmonious whole, an expression of a more refined and planned beauty than was ever before conceived. There was an ecstatic response to the bedroom at Hill House in a famous German art review at the time: 'the exotic bloom of a strange plant, not made but grown, not sensuous but chaste, not floating like a dream, but firm and decisive like the poetic vision of a fact that is expressed in the

The main bedroom at Hill House, Helensburgh

only possible art form . . .' Indeed, so much has the interior design become a work of art in its own right that even a minor clashing element such as a book of the wrong colour might disturb the delicate interplay. In fact, it is hard to imagine such rooms in everyday use for they are best viewed when clear of the traces of human occupation like private temples for aesthetic meditation.

Not surprisingly, such an uncompromising quest for artistic beauty was not generally understood by the hard-headed Glaswegians

Hill House, Helensburgh

The drawing-room at Hill House, Helensburgh

of the day; it was in the cultural centres of the new movement in Europe, notably Vienna, that Mackintosh became recognised as the revolutionary master designer and architect that he certainly was. At home it was a different story. His popular reputation rested largely on the stunning series of tearooms he designed for a Miss Cranston. Without the unfailing support of the head-master of the Glasgow School of Art, Francis Newbery, it is unlikely that Mackintosh would have made even the limited impact at

The library at the Glasgow School of Art

home that he did, and he would not have had the chance to execute his design for what is without doubt the most significant single building in Glasgow, if not the whole of Scotland.

Mackintosh's new Glasgow School of Art design of 1896, together with the revisions for the west wing added in 1907-9, aroused little comment at first but has since come to be acclaimed as a pioneer of the 'modern style' in Europe and a landmark in architectural history. The beauty of the concept and the dramatic tension of the building reside in the way form flows quite naturally from

function. There are no tricks or contrived stylistic devices imposed indiscriminately. The library, with its soaring pillars of stained wood like a pine forest, the airy spaciousness of the studios and the magnificent windows of the north and west fronts are but the highlights of an integrated design. As the client of Hill House noted of Mackintosh: 'With him the practical purpose came first. The pleasing design followed of itself as it were.'

Sadly, Mackintosh did not succeed in converting his compatriots to his way of thinking about architecture, and even today he is often remembered more as the exotic Art Nouveau designer of some spectacular

tearooms and the chief mover of the rather frivolous *fin de siècle* 'Glasgow style' than as a serious architect. His lack of recognition at home eventually broke his spirit, and he left Glasgow in 1914 to seek his future in the south. In London he fared no better and in 1923 he moved to France and abandoned architecture altogether in favour of his first love of painting water-colours. But he died in 1928 of cancer of the tongue before he was able to exhibit his work, and even after his death a true evaluation of his genius was not forthcoming. In 1933 the entire contents of his studio, including thirty-one paintings and some items of original furniture, were estimated to be worth in all only £88 16s. 2d.

Thanks largely to the posthumous international acclaim he has at last received, Mackintosh is today highly appreciated in Glasgow as well, where there are several examples of his work as shrines to his memory. The Charles Rennie Mackintosh Society has its headquarters in Queen's Cross, his only church in the city. The Hunterian Art Gallery has reconstructed in the finest possible manner the interior of a Victorian terraced house which the young Mackintosh and his wife Margaret lovingly converted for their own use. Described by a contemporary as 'the loveliest lodging in the world' it is also the most intimate relic of a man who was at least a generation ahead of his time.

Given the high status he now enjoys it is surprising to reflect that all of his major work was accomplished within an extraordinarily brief creative period from 1896 to 1906. Mackintosh was like a rare blossom that flowers and dies before its effect can be properly perceived. In his lifetime he was considered as a futuristic and revolutionary architect but in retrospect it is possible to see how one of the great strengths of his building was his adherence to the spirit of the native Scottish tradition with its unfailing instinct for practical and pleasingly simple solutions to the functions demanded of architecture.

West aspect of the Glasgow School of Art

The Fruits of Success

Such was the wealth and energy of Victorian Glasgow that it was still contributing to the Scottish national heritage in the early 1980s. The opening of the Burrell Collection in 1983 may be traced directly back to the vision of a man whose fortunes were rooted in the prosperity of nineteenth-century Glasgow. William Burrell, an exceptionally shrewd businessman, was a typical product of his age. By the outbreak of the Great War he had made an immense profit by skilfully manoeuvring between the booms and slumps of the shipping business, so that in 1916 he was able to retire and devote the rest of his long life (1861-1958) to the amassing of one of the most remarkable private fine art collections in the world. It was this priceless accumulation of some 6,000 individual items that Burrell donated to the City of Glasgow in 1944.

The Burrell Collection is naturally strongest in the areas closest to the heart of the collector himself. Burrell's passion for mediaeval artefacts such as sculpture, tapestries, stained glass and oak furniture places him firmly in the ranks of the Scottish Baronialists. Indeed, it was an early dream of his to have his residence built on the ruins of Newark Castle in Fife. When business interests compelled him to live in Glasgow he employed the architect Lorimer to convert the interior of his neoclassical house in Great Western Terrace, designed by Alexander 'Greek' Thomson no less, into a Gothic scene appropriate to his mediaeval fittings and furnishings. And on his retirement in 1916 he purchased Hutton Castle in Berwickshire, where it took eleven years of complex conversion work before he was ready to move into his oak-panelled Baronial paradise hung with original tapestries and fitted with some exquisite pieces of stained glass. Just how potent was the effect can be seen from the original interiors of the dining-room, drawing-room and hall of Hutton Castle, which have been faithfully reconstructed in the new Burrell Collection; it was one of the strict conditions of the bequest that this should be done.

But these and the other magnificent items of stone architecture, such as the heraldic portal from Hornby Castle, do not dictate the style of the modern building, which is a splendid mixture of pink Dumfriesshire stone, steel, timber and glass which provides a magical interplay with the woodland setting. In accordance with Burrell's wishes it is not a museum-type institution but a novel accommodation for displaying works of art to their best effect.

As for the collection itself, Burrell's taste ranged far and wide, embracing the cultures

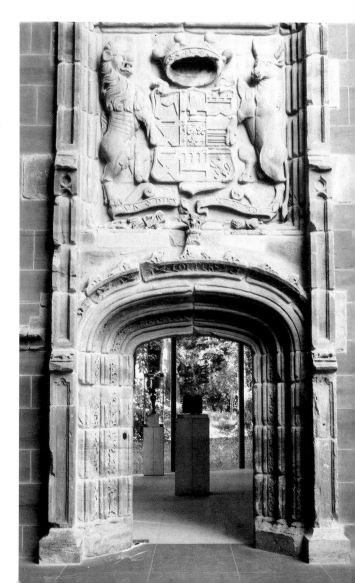

Portal from Hornby Castle in the Burrell Collection, Glasgow

of the Far East and the Middle East as well as Europe. It is perhaps significant that there is no reference to objects of Scottish antiquarian interest, in fact almost an avoidance of the national heritage, which reflects the internationalism of Glasgow in the nineteenth century. Although Burrell as a collector was all too often guided by his business instincts for a bargain rather than by true artistic inspiration, he did manage to put together a comprehensive collection which yet leans markedly towards the Middle Ages and seems to avoid anything avant-garde.

Quite apart from the beauty of the exhibits, the Burrell Collection may be regarded as an

Interaction of glass, steel and stone at the Burrell Collection

expression of the energy and achievements of Victorian and Edwardian Glasgow. In the 1890s when William Burrell was in his early manhood, Glasgow was not just wealthy but also cosmopolitan in outlook and had some real claim as an important market for fine art. A number of Burrell's contemporaries were also collectors, and the city's art dealers included men such as Alexander Reid, who was known and respected in the major centres of Europe. The 1901 Glasgow International Exhibition showed the scope of the city's massive investment in fine art, with Burrell alone loaning more than two hundred works. Thus the Burrell Collection is a continuation of a triumphant Glasgow tradition, and it is satisfying that the city in

which the Burrell fortune was made should inherit the unique artistic legacy on which it was expended. The fruits of past success are there for future generations to admire. The Burrell Collection, together with its outstanding building, is also a memorial to the man who shunned publicity and always stated that the collection is more important than the collector. In accordance with this attitude Burrell had no intention of his home at Hutton Castle becoming a shrine-cum-museum after his death. Quite the opposite occurred, for Burrell had the Baronial interiors removed during the last years of his life and Hutton Castle has since remained abandoned as a gutted and gloomy ruin.

Interior view of the Burrell Collection

GAZETTEER   7

Castles and Country Houses
1 Ayton
2 Balmoral
3 Brodick
4 Dunrobin
5 The Hill House
6 Hill of Tarvit
7 Kinloch
8 Manderston
9 Torosay

Churches
10 Crathie
11 Croick
12 Queen's Cross, Glasgow
13 St Vincent Street, Glasgow

Civic Architecture
14 City Chambers, Glasgow
15 Town House, Aberdeen

Commercial Buildings
16 Gardner's Warehouse, Glasgow
17 Merchants' House, Glasgow
18 Stock Exchange, Glasgow
19 Templeton's Carpet Factory, Glasgow

Educational and Cultural Institutions
20 Art Gallery and Museum, Glasgow
21 The Burrell Collection, Glasgow
22 Fettes College
23 Glasgow School of Art
24 Hunterian Art Gallery, Glasgow
25 Marischal College, Aberdeen
26 Mitchell Library, Glasgow
27 National Museum of Antiquities, Edinburgh
28 People's Palace, Glasgow
29 Royal Scottish Museum, Edinburgh
30 Scotland Street School, Glasgow
31 University of Glasgow

Industrial
32 Easdale Island
33 Forth Rail Bridge
34 Prestongrange Mining Museum
35 Tay Rail Bridge

Historical Sites
36 Queen's View, Loch Lomond
37 Queen's View, Loch Tummel

Monuments and Memorials
38 Glasgow Necropolis
39 Livingstone National Memorial
40 McCaig Tower, Oban
41 Scott Monument, Edinburgh
42 Wallace Monument, Stirling

Rural
43 Angus Folk Museum, Glamis
44 Colbost Black-house, Skye
45 Highland Folk Museum, Kingussie
46 Kilmuir Croft Museum, Skye
47 Lewis Black-house, Arnol
48 Lhaidhay Caithness Croft
49 Old Skye Crofter's House, Luib
50 Shawbost Folk Museum, Lewis
51 Shetland Croft House Museum
52 Skye Water Mill
53 Strathnaver Museum

Miscellaneous
54 The Tenement House, Glasgow

Gardens
55 Inverewe Gardens
56 Kibble Palace, Glasgow Botanic Gardens
57 Palm House, Royal Botanic Gardens, Edinburgh

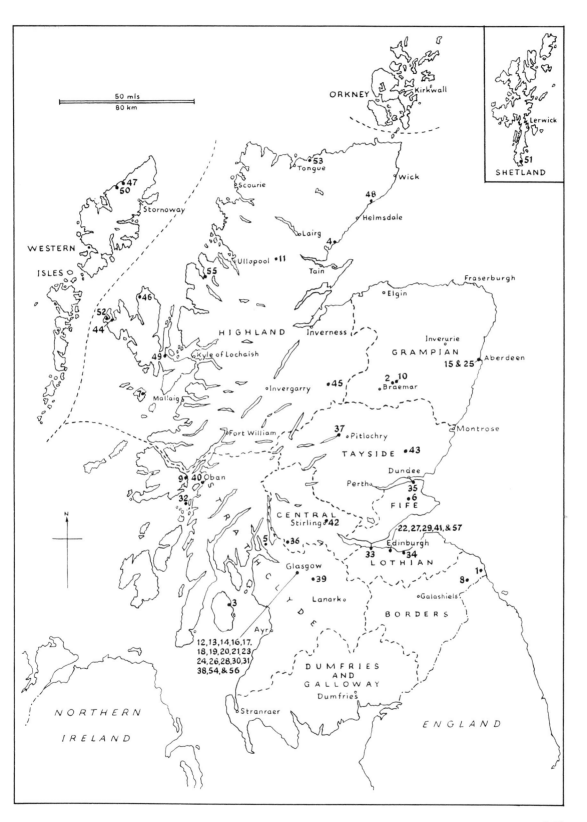

50 mls
80 km

ORKNEY ·Kirkwall

SHETLAND ·Lerwick

·51

·53
Tongue

·Scourie

·47
·50

Stornoway

WESTERN

ISLES

·11
·Ullapool

·55

·46

52
44

49
·Kyle of Lochalsh

Mallaig

·Wick

48

·Helmsdale

·Lairg

4·

Tain

·Elgin

HIGHLAND

Inverness

·Invergarry

Fort William

·45

GRAMPIAN

Inverurie
○

15 & 25

·Aberdeen

2· ·10
Braemar

·Montrose

37·
·Pitlochry

TAYSIDE

·43

9· 40·Oban

32·

CENTRAL
Stirling·42

5·

·36

Glasgow

·39

·3

Ayr·

12,13,14,16,17.
18,19,20,21,23
24,26,28,30,31
38,54,& 56

Lanark○

NORTHERN

IRELAND

Dundee

Perth○

35·
·6
FIFE

22,27,29,41,& 57

Edinburgh
○
33· ·34
LOTHIAN

·Galashiels

BORDERS

DUMFRIES
AND
GALLOWAY
Dumfries○

·Stranraer

1·

8·

ENGLAND

N

247

Exploring Scotland's Heritage

Nearly all of the sites and monuments mentioned in this book are easily accessible by car, although some require a short walk along indicated paths. The map locations given with the gazetteer at the end of each section are intended only as a rough guide. It is assumed that visitors to Scotland will consult the relevant Ordnance Survey maps in the 1:50,000 series for precise location of out-of-the-way places. For general purposes there is the booklet *1001 Things to See*, published by the Scottish Tourist Board, with a useful companion map which clearly marks most places of historic interest. These publications are available from bookshops and tourist information centres throughout Scotland as well as from: Scottish Tourist Board, 23 Ravelston Terrace, Edinburgh EH4 3EU.

The Scottish Development Department publishes a booklet entitled *Scotland's Historic Buildings and Monuments*. This directory of sites open to the public is a listing complete with outline maps of those places in the care of the Historic Buildings and Monuments Directorate. This organisation also operates a membership scheme 'Friends of Scottish Monuments' which, for a modest fee, gives free access for a year. The family card is particularly good value and the cost can be easily recouped in the course of a couple of fairly intensive weeks on the heritage trail. The sites in question are generally well indicated with distinctive grey and blue signposts and information panels. All the major monuments such as the castles and abbeys are described and illustrated in a remarkable series of individual booklets of a high standard. Further information may be obtained from: Historic Buildings and Monuments, Scottish Development Department, PO Box 157, Edinburgh EH3 7QD.

The National Trust for Scotland has in its care a surprising diversity of places, not just castles, country houses and gardens, but also huge tracts of wild landscape and entire islands as well as tiny cottages and even a complete town, i.e. Culross. The Trust publishes in addition to the many guides to individual places an annual *Guide to Over 100 Properties* which is on sale as well as supplied to members. Further information may be obtained from: The National Trust for Scotland, 5 Charlotte Square, Edinburgh EH2 4DU.

The Royal Commission on the Ancient and Historical Monuments of Scotland is currently publishing through HMSO a series of regional guides under the heading of 'Exploring Scotland's Heritage'. These well-presented and instructive books provide a wealth of historical information as well as National Grid References which are especially useful for prehistoric sites off the beaten track. A further practical feature of these books is the grading of the accessibility of each site for the handicapped. Further information may be obtained from HMSO or through booksellers.

Bibliography

Clapperton, Chalmers M. (ed.), *Scotland: A New Study*, David & Charles, 1983.

Cruden, Stewart, *Scottish Abbeys*, HMSO Edinburgh, 1960.

Cruden, Stewart, *The Scottish Castle*, Spurbooks, 1981.

Dickinson, W. Croft, and Duncan, *Scotland from the Earliest Times to 1603*, Clarendon Press, 1977.

Dunbar, John G., *The Architecture of Scotland*, Batsford, 1978.

Dunbar, J. Telfer, *The Costume of Scotland*, Batsford, 1981.

Feachem, Richard, *Guide to Prehistoric Scotland*, Batsford, 1977.

Fenwick, Hubert, *Scotland's Historic Buildings*, Robert Hale, 1974.

Grimble, Ian, *Highland Man*, Highlands and Islands Development Board, 1980.

Maclean, Fitzroy, *A Concise History of Scotland*, Thames & Hudson, 1981.

Millman, Richard N., *The Making of the Scottish Landscape*, Batsford, 1975.

Muir, Richard, *Shell Guide to Reading the Celtic Landscapes*, Michael Joseph, 1985.

Piggott, Stuart, and Henderson, *Scotland Before History*, Edinburgh University Press, 1982.

Prebble, John, *The Lion in the North*, Penguin, 1973.

Prentice, Robert (ed.), *The National Trust for Scotland Guide*, Jonathan Cape, 1981.

Ritchie, Graham and Anna, *Scotland: Archaeology and Early History*, Thames & Hudson, 1985.

Royal Commission on the Ancient and Historical Monuments of Scotland, *Exploring Scotland's Heritage (Regional Series)*, HMSO.

Simpson, W. Douglas, *The Ancient Stones of Scotland*, Robert Hale, 1968.

Stormouth Darling, James (ed.), *Shell Guide: Northern Scotland and Islands*, Michael Joseph, 1987.

Wainwright, F. T. (ed.), *The Problem of the Picts*, Melven Press, 1981.

Williams, Ronald, *The Lords of the Isles*, Chatto & Windus, 1984.

Index

Page numbers in *italic* refer to illustrations